What People are Saying About
Tips and Tools for
GETTING *thru* TO KIDS

"Phillip Mountrose's first book *Getting Thru to Kids: Problem Solving with Children Ages 6-18* brought new thinking forward. Now *Tips and Tools for Getting Thru to Kids* offers many how-to and how-come techniques that work wonderfully well. The secret of this book is that it helps us adults learn along with the kids as we establish true and meaningful communication."

- Gerald Brong
Educational Quality Consultant

"Phillip Mountrose has again written a book that will significantly help and uplift parents, educators, and counselors. His common-sense approach offers a wealth of exceptional material that can be put to immediate use. A great resource!"

- Ric Teagarden,
Superintendent of Schools and Radio Host

"To get through to your kids, you have to get through to your own issues. As the mother of four young children, I know how difficult this can be at times. This book is an insightful, creative resource for anyone who wants to improve communication with their children, or any other family members for that matter. Highly recommended."

- Lisa Roberts, author of
How to Raise A Family & A Career Under One Roof

"Phillip Mountrose's deep understanding of children is translated wonderfully into this work. His book is a valuable resource for those dealing with kids from the time they enter school until the time they graduate years later. *Tips and Tools for Getting Thru to Kids* not only helps readers better understand children, it also helps them to better understand themselves. An accomplishment that is well worth studying."

- Michael Gurian, author of
The Wonder of Boys and *A Fine Young Man*

"Read it...think about it...learn from it. Phillip Mountrose has great advice to help us all through the parenting morass. There are better ways than the ways we were brought up!"

- D. Honnold, author of *San Jose with Kids*,
co-author of *Sacramento Family Resource Guide*

"Phillip Mountrose has put together powerful insights with a wide range of great techniques that anyone who lives or works with children can easily use. His book clearly shows how self-improvement complements helping children improve."

- Rick Pierce, author of
How to Help an ADD Child Succeed in Life

"This book offers a great opportunity for personal growth and awareness while increasing more effective interactions with children. Phillip Mountrose provides practical and innovative solutions for parents/educators that will help children develop skills for well-balanced and self-fulfilled lives."

- Dana I. McKnight, Social Worker, Educator

"Phillip Mountrose powerfully conveys how we can relate more to children and better understand ourselves. I am glad I had the opportunity to read this book, and I know the children and teenagers in my life will be glad I did too."

- Sean Clancy, Special Education Teacher

"*Tips and Tools for Getting Thru to Kids* offers powerful solutions for those of us working with children and teenagers. Phillip Mountrose's approach offers sensible and dynamic ways to take our relationships to the next level."

- Barbara Silver, Principal

"Candid, thought-provoking and refreshingly readable. I recommend to all parents and educators the concepts described in this invaluable guide for human growth."

- Barbara Agnell, Clinical Director
Paradise Oaks Youth Services, L.C.S.W.

"This book is a must read for all parents. Phillip has written a book that gives parents and those working with children clearly defined guidelines on how to communicate with kids – which is after all, the foundation of effective parenting. I read numerous self-help books, along with many parenting books, and I see this one as a combination of both. I gleaned self-awareness along with many excellent ideas. I have added this book to my recommended reading list."

- Shirley King, Parenting Columnist and Host of *Kid Talk*

Tips and Tools for
GETTING *thru* TO KIDS

Phillip Mountrose

Holistic Communications
Sacramento, California

Published by: Holistic Communications
                P.O. Box 41152
                Sacramento, CA 95841-0152 USA
                Fax: 916-972-0237; E-mail: kids@gettingthru.org

ISBN: 0-9653787-4-8
Library of Congress Catalog Card Number: 98-93530

Publisher's Cataloging-in-Publication
    (*Provided by Quality Books Inc.*)
Mountrose, Phillip.
Tips and Tools for Getting thru to kids / Phillip Mountrose.
--1st ed.
p. cm. – (Getting thru)
Includes biographical references and index.
Preassigned LCCN: 98-93530
ISBN 0-9653787-4-8
1. Child rearing. 2. Communication in the family 3. Parenting. 4. Moral education.
Title. II. Title: Tips and tools for getting thru to kids
HQ769.M68 1999   649'.7
            QBI98-1342

To the children in the world
Whose love and laughter
Have enriched us in so many ways.

Acknowledgments

This book is about the journey through childhood and on through adulthood. Part of the journey for me has included writing this book. In writing this material, I have been fortunate to cross paths with others who have offered me generous and insightful help.

I would like to thank the following people for their input: Briana Finley, Marian Hakata, Dana McKnight, Dierdre Honnold, Sean Clancy, Sandra Rhymer, Barbara Agnell, Debbie Dohnt, Barbara Silver, and Robert Juran. Also, I would like to add special thanks to my wife Jane, who helps me in innumerable ways.

I would also like to thank the many children and adults who have crossed my path and taught me what I needed to know.

Table of Contents

Table of Tools

Introduction

Have you ever wished kids came with a manual? Perhaps part of the challenge is that children are far more complex than any machine. In sorting matters out, we should remember that our parents didn't have any manual for us either.

Not so long ago we were children ourselves, and it was someone else's role to take care of us. Now it is our turn to help children. We share many experiences with children, including passing through the same developmental stages they undergo. Paradoxically, we can see ourselves in the children around us while realizing that they are individuals too, unique with their own individual paths.

Despite a legacy of research and books about our role with children, there is still much missing from our understanding of who we are, where we have come from, and where we are headed. We are given the awesome role of helping the young, while lacking certain knowledge and insights about our own childhood origins and how they affect us as adults. To paraphrase a saying, we have met the mystery and it is us!

This book seeks to find some of the missing pieces. It explores childhood, where it ends and where adulthood begins, and how the child and adult can best co-exist. Each stage influences what follows it: Our childhood experiences affect the teenager, who in turn affects the adult. To continue the cycle, we as adults affect the children in our lives. At a deeper level, we still have childhood parts that lie within, those younger parts of ourselves that have shaped (or misshaped) our character and personality. Our inner child consciousness holds a key to our own development, as well as to the development of the children we have in our care.

HELPING YOURSELF SO YOU CAN HELP CHILDREN

Let's consider how communication is traditionally approached. Most child-care books divide their audience: On the one hand there is the adult readership, and on the other hand there are the children whom the adults will help by reading the material. However unknowingly, this approach can create separation between children and grown-ups. Often the child-care author's message is: I will offer material for you, so you can better manage and relate to kids.

It seems that something is missing in this orientation. What's absent in the picture is the adult's responsibility for himself or herself. In other words, when giving kids directions and criticisms, we too often forget to see how well we do in those same areas. To offer a few examples: If we want kids to have better boundaries, how healthy are our own boundaries? If we want kids to redress their own errors, how do we handle our own mistakes? In child-care books, this crucial missing piece of self-reflection is often embodied in the division between an author writing to "you" (the adult reader) about "them" (the children in your life).

To be sure, there are distinctions between adult and child. Adults have accumulated more experience. They have more knowledge in certain areas. They have gone through more stages of life than children have. These differences, though, can easily be emphasized at the expense of what adults share in common with children.

What we have in common bonds us together, helping us to understand that our own self-development relates directly to helping children develop.

For instance, by the time kids are age five or six, talking to kids is basically the same thing as talking to adults, as Suzette Haden Elgin notes in *The Gentle Art of Communicating with Kids*.

Fortunately, the many vital links between adult and child are beginning to be addressed in works such as Hendrix and Hunt's *Giving the Love That Heals* and the emotional literacy movement initiated by Daniel Goleman's *Emotional Intelligence: Why It Can Matter More Than IQ*.

In trying to go beyond this unconscious split between adult and child, I consider you, as a reader of this book, as more than a helper and communicator to children. This material applies to you as well as to the younger beings in your life. This book will build on your wealth of experience and wisdom, giving you more knowledge and tools that will improve your life as you help children. By examining in yourself this book's topics—trust, honesty, courage, limit-setting, listening skills, and emotional awareness—you will be able to communicate with children more from your heart, rather than simply giving kids advice and directions.

FULFILLING OUR POTENTIAL

We sometimes fear that looking inward will open a Pandora's Box of untold miseries. Actually, looking within does not aggravate problems, but simply helps us process and integrate incomplete parts of ourselves in order to live a better, fuller life. Our inward search helps us discover the unwanted baggage of our life, such as negative emotions, limiting beliefs, and harsh judgments of others and ourselves. By probing what's underneath, we can then choose to give up our own limitations, popping the bubble of our self-imposed prison. Understanding ourselves better, we are then freer to fulfill our own potential, which includes loving ourselves and our children.

Inside ourselves also lie our own strengths, areas where we excel with ourselves and with others. These parts deserve to be acknowledged, reinforced, and developed too. Looking within, we discover a wonderful, loving person who has much to offer. The more in touch we become with ourselves, the more in touch we can be with others. Then helping children is not such an overwhelming task, a role that we may agonize over or glibly describe by saying, "Everything is fine." As we connect more with ourselves and our kids, problems become opportunities for learning and growth. Life becomes filled with more fun and joy. We are freer to grow together, in our own way, at our own rate.

Ultimately the secret is revealed: It is not what we do for kids, it is what we do with ourselves, and the rest naturally follows. To this end, refer to the quote at the start of this Introduction.

> *Confucius, the ancient Chinese sage, points out that educating children brings success for a lifetime.*

Implicit in this vision is the value of children receiving an education. Those dealing with children, such as caregivers and educators are the instructors, who must have knowledge about themselves as well as the world in which kids will be raised.

As we take more responsibility for ourselves, we naturally know how to be more responsible with kids. As we learn to trust ourselves more, we can better teach, demonstrate, and live that trust with children. As we develop healthy boundaries in our own lives, we know how to set appropriate limits with children. As we grow, the kids in our lives are free to fulfill their potential, supported by our own self-knowledge to appropriately guide them.

A woman once brought her ailing son to Mahatma Gandhi for help. After examining him and asking questions about his diet, Gandhi requested that the woman bring him back in a week. When she returned, Gandhi told her that the son should restrict sugar from his diet. The woman responded, "Why didn't you tell us that on the first visit?" Gandhi responded, "At that time, Madam, I was still eating sugar myself."

Dealing with our own issues makes us effective communicators and healers. Self-knowledge also brings self-fulfillment.

WHAT THIS BOOK HAS IN STORE FOR YOU

This volume has three basic parts to enrich both you and the children in your life.

Part One is "Helping Yourself, Helping Kids." Understanding and developing yourself is crucial to yourself and to helping children. The kids around you reflect your strengths and weaknesses. As you develop yourself, you pave the way for those younger people whom you are in a position to help.

Part Two, "Getting to the Basics," transitions from working with yourself to more directly working with children. It includes gaining trust, exploring feelings, improving listening, and establishing boundaries. This is still a two-way street, with your success of helping kids based on your own self-knowledge and self-respect.

Part Three maps out ways of "Making Growth Choices." This section includes a collection of insights, exercises, and approaches that can spur growth for both you and children. These chapters suggest ways for you to help kids: improve honesty, deal with remorse, assess courage and risk-taking, stop complaining, and have appropriate consequences. The book concludes by discussing how important increasing awareness is for us and our children.

HOW TO USE THIS BOOK

As the title of this volume indicates, there are many practical and powerful tools offered in this book. To be exact, there are 25 interactive tools. These approaches come in the form of exercises, checklists, journaling, fill-in-the-blank sentences, and affirmations. In the following section, there is a listing and summary of the tools offered in this book. As Confucius advised long ago, "I hear and I forget; I see and I remember; I do and I understand." In light of recent research, the first part of this observation—"I hear and I forget"—might be revised to note that some people learn better through the hearing rather than the visual mode. In any event, the second part of Confucius' advice holds true: You will gain invaluable self-knowledge by putting these tools into practice.

Consider the following ways to use the tips and tools in this book:

- After reading the book for an overview, return to the parts you feel will give you the most benefit, the sections you are most drawn to read.

- You may want to use a similar approach in using the interactive tools: Selectively spend time on the ones you consider most important, rather than hurriedly trying to cover everything in the book.

This book is designed as an easy-to-use resource that can yield practical and profound understanding for you and your kids. The tips extend your knowledge, helping you to find better ways to improve the communication skills you already possess. The tools help self-development, raising your own awareness and enhancing your relationship with yourself and your children.

TOOLS FOR BREAKTHROUGH COMMUNICATION

In order to more easily reference the 25 tools in this book, here is an overview of the complete list. The tools are grouped according to the part of the book in which they appear.

PART 1: Helping Yourself, Helping Kids

★ Tool 1: Affirmations for Growth
Brief sayings that can spur growth and help fulfill your children's potential—and your own.

★ Tool 2: Developing an Attitude of Gratitude
A gratitude list to appreciate more of what you have in life, helping move past the hurt and loss.

PART 2: Getting to the Basics

★ Tool 3: Establishing Trust
Practical methods to help kids establish trust, a vital component for their developmental growth.

★ Tool 4: Jump-starting the Discussion Checklist
Various key points to help you initiate discussions with young people; this checklist can be particularly helpful when they are resistant to talking.

★ Tool 5: Phrasing for Validation
Helpful phrases for you to validate children's thinking.

★ Tool 6: Phrasing for Empathy
Helpful phrases for you to empathize with kids' feelings.

★ Tool 7: Beginning the Feeling Exploration
Various ways to bring out children's recognition and expression of feelings.

PART 3: Making Growth Choices

★ **Tool 8: Defusing Anger**
A powerful technique for kids and adults to find the underlying needs that anger covers, concluding with an action plan to resolve the situation.

★ **Tool 9: Using "I Statements" to Express Anger**
Simple "I statements" direct your feelings so children can hear the message you truly want to give.

★ **Tool 10: Defining Boundaries**
Strategies to help children recognize and establish healthy boundaries.

★ **Tool 11: Turning Telling into Asking**
Clear-cut questions to increase kids' listening and thinking ability.

★ **Tool 12: Phrases and Tips to Avoid Lecturing**
Practical ways to communicate without resorting to the negative practice of lecturing.

★ **Tool 13: Learning from Our Mistakes**
A straightforward approach on how to use mistakes—both children's and adults'—as learning tools.

★ **Tool 14: Affirmations for Healthy Remorse**
Sayings to identify and develop remorse for both children and adults.

★ **Tool 15: Acting as an Honorable Person**
A technique to help young people correct situations and feel good about themselves, rather than be defensive and blaming.

★ **Tool 16: Honesty and Its Benefits**
A question-and-answer approach for helping kids understand the results of honesty and dishonesty.

★ **Tool 17: Catching Children Being Honest**
A way to reinforce children when they tell the truth, and teach them how to get in the practice of truth-telling.

★ **Tool 18: Exploring Courage**
An inventory to define and evaluate your courage.

★ **Tool 19: Courage to Play the Fool**
Ways to help children take healthy risks and avoid harmful ones, using the archetypal idea of the fool.

★ **Tool 20: Effective-Consequences Checklist**
Key points to consider when using consequences with kids.

★ **Tool 21: Finding the Lesson and the Alternatives**
An easy-to-use process to prevent and deal with problems.

★ **Tool 22: Asked and Answered**
A simple technique to stop children's repeated requests and nagging.

★ **Tool 23: Developing Consistency**
A method to evaluate and develop consistent responses with children, helping to provide them with a stable environment.

★ **Tool 24: The "I Know" Technique**

A quick and simple response to acknowledge children and avoid power struggles.

★ **Tool 25: Improving Your Results**

Ways to evaluate and strengthen the relationships you have with young people.

As you may have gathered, the tools in the book can be practically applied to a wide range of subjects. A particular tool can be used for your own self-improvement, children's advancement, or both.

Here is a sample interactive tool excerpted from the chapter "Learning to Listen":

★ SAMPLE TOOL ★
Phrasing for Validation

To develop listening skills, you can use these phrases to validate the child's words:

- I understand that.
- It makes sense.
- It's important for you.
- You have a point there.

Consider using one or more of these phrases, or something comparable, in your next meeting with the kids in your life. To get started, I will give an example and then you can follow by finding your own example.

- "I can understand that you want to stay out that late with your friends." Now it's your turn: "I can understand that..."

- "It makes sense that you would want to buy that dress." Your turn: "It makes sense that..."

- "It's important for you to have that computer game." Your turn: "It's important for you..."

- "You have a point about my taking you to the mall." Your turn: "You have a point..."

Sometimes you will need to repeat the tools to gain the desired results. At other times, it is wise to move on to a different approach. To develop a sense of timing on how to proceed, follow your intuition along with learning from your experience.

YOU ARE MAKING A DIFFERENCE

The fact that you are reading this book says some positive things about you: You are interested in and committed to helping children. You are also interested in improving yourself and your communication skills. As you activate your own growth and assimilate what you have learned, you help pave the way for yourself and those around you.

This book is intended to be more than a resource for you. Although it can be a valuable reference, *Tips and Tools for Getting Thru to Kids* is not meant to be an authoritative text that holds the answers outside of you. Rather, the information and tools can serve as a catalyst for discovering your own inner wisdom and resources. The material you choose to assimilate then becomes transformed inside you. As you discover more of the light within you, your own understanding becomes a torch that will shine and be passed on to children for generations to come.

Part 1

HELPING YOURSELF, HELPING KIDS

"When Abraham Lincoln was your age,"
the father told his son, "he used to walk 10 miles
every day to get to school." "Really?" the kid said.
"Well, when he was your *age, he was president."*

- JOE CLARO

CHAPTER ONE

Taking Communication to the Next Level

Improving our relationships with kids is based both on valuing our strengths and on dealing with our weaknesses. Yet we sometimes forget how valuable we are, becoming our own worst enemies when it comes to our strengths and weaknesses. We often take for granted our strengths, while we avoid facing our weaknesses.

Sometimes we are very sensitive to anything that could be considered criticism of our parenting, educating, and relating to kids. We all know there are weaknesses in ourselves and in our relationships, but it can be hard to admit our humanness in today's culture. Like a young child ourselves, we fear being caught, reprimanded, and shamed by others, as we try to avoid being identified as deficient and less than capable in our role of helping children. Ironically, these vulnerable areas hold the keys to our own growth, the very material that will help ourselves and the kids in our lives.

Now is a good time to value ourselves and affirm our own growth process, which in turn helps our children grow.

★ TOOL 1 ★
Affirmations For Growth

Affirmations are condensed messages that help bring out the best in ourselves. Forming the words for affirmations communicates with our auditory sense, whether we say it aloud or hear it internally. The spoken or unspoken messages may evoke visual images, which can further strengthen their impact. Such positive phrases train our subconscious mind to attract success.

Affirmations state how lovable and capable we are. They connect with our wholeness, our self-worth, and our ability to improve. Affirmations help us fulfill our potential, our future self. Here are some positive messages for you and your children:

- I am fulfilling my potential.

- I face my difficulties and learn and grow from them.

- My love conquers my fears.

- Challenges are opportunities for growth.

- I enjoy today and all the success it brings.

- I can get my needs met.

- My life is becoming more joyful in every way.

- I am here for a reason.

- I am making a difference.

- I am making a positive impact on those around me.

- I am making healthy decisions about my life.

You might want to commit some of the affirmations to memory, considering ways of applying them to your life and your children's lives, such as posting them prominently somewhere. You and your children can write your own affirmations, using your own language.

At first there might be resistance to the affirmations, as old negative patterns surface. You can acknowledge these obstacles and then put forth a positive affirmation that incorporates the stumbling blocks. For instance, if you or the child feel that tiredness accounts for poor work habits, you can affirm: "Even though I am tired, I can find ways to rest and do my work."

In formulating affirmations, you also want to focus on the positive. For example, "I can have more fun while I learn" instead of "School isn't that boring." Or "I can be honest" rather than "I won't lie."

Affirmations are particularly effective when used in combination with other tools presented throughout this book.

Affirmations plant positive seeds that can change your life.

They are a wonderful resource for making your present life more enjoyable and attracting a desirable future. To conclude, here is one more affirmation: "Using affirmations creates positive change in my life."

★ TOOL 2 ★
Developing an Attitude of Gratitude

To further create a positive future, consider how to develop more gratitude in your life. When was the last time you smiled at someone? When did you last hug someone? Appreciating others can be made into a daily practice, rather than something to do only during a birthday or special event. Life itself is a gift we have all received.

Have yourself and your kids make a gratitude list, which can include people, positive events, skills and talents, and the Earth with all that it provides us. Try the following exercise.

1. Brainstorm a list of things in your life for which you are grateful.

2. Write down a way you can show your gratitude today and every day.

3. What benefits will you receive from increasing your gratitude?

An interesting, related study occurred in a college psychology course. The professor divided his 200 students into three groups: One group listed five things they were grateful for; the second listed five things that irritated them; the third listed major events of the week. Ten weeks later, the "grateful" group reported feeling healthier and happier, accomplishing more toward their goals, and even exercising more. The third group, which had the option of reporting good or bad events, generally gravitated to focusing on the negative. Their responses tended to match the second "hassled" group, both of which evaluated themselves as less happy and healthy, and further away from meeting their goals than the "grateful" group.

You might want to use the gratitude tool at the beginning of each week to start things off right.

Gratitude is a wonderful, uplifting practice, and it clearly beats dwelling on what goes wrong in our lives. At the same time, we need to constructively deal with our problems so we can heal ourselves and further help our children.

EVERYONE HAS PROBLEMS TO SOLVE

At some of my bookstore presentations, I came across some revealing responses from people who were not interested in my previous book *Getting Thru to Kids: Problem Solving with Children Ages 6 to 18*. What was quite telling, and sometimes humorous, were the reasons some adults said they were not interested in the material. Here are some examples.

"My children don't have problems. They are doing very well."

"I have good kids. We're fine."

"Our daughter is 16, and if we haven't gotten it by now, we might as well forget it."

"I'm not interested in the book. But speak to my husband; he needs it."

"I'm the father. I'm not really the parent."

This last comment reminds me of a cartoon showing a young boy asking his father, who is reading the newspaper in his armchair, "What's a man's role in getting through to kids?" He responds, without looking up from his paper, "Go ask your mother."

Other common responses to my book came from people who said they knew *others* who could benefit from learning the communication skills covered in the material. Sometimes kids told me their parents could really use a book with a title like *Getting Thru to Kids: Problem Solving with Children Ages 6 to 18.* The parents usually responded nervously, fidgeted, and departed.

Another time, a ten-year-old girl walking alongside her mom spotted my *Getting Thru to Kids* book. The youngster exclaimed to her mother, "Oh, Mom, look at this book!" The mother looked over to me and said, "We're not interested," and quickly took her daughter's hand and moved on.

Especially if you have a relatively well-adjusted family, you know that working with life's challenges creates stability and nurtures growth. When the problems inevitably do arise, you will want to have the best resources available, bolstering your awareness in times of crisis.

Yet adults, like children, sometimes have trouble asking for help. John Bradshaw wrote in *The Family:* "We will resist the knowledge we most deeply desire. Language, ego defenses, denials, delusions, family system and cultural roles keep us from higher consciousness." The good news is that higher consciousness awaits us all, patiently residing within as it holds the key to our potential. Our inner wisdom will help us to transform weaknesses into strengths.

Many times we equate having family problems with shame and defeat. From this point of view, having a problem shows weakness, failure, and helplessness. Yet don't we all have areas that are unclear and uncomfortable in our lives? And as the saying goes, running from problems is a sure way to run into problems.

Receiving help and healing ourselves and our families is nurturing and leads to self-improvement.

Surely this is a better cycle than one of hiding problems and feeling ashamed by our difficulties.

EVERYONE CAN LEARN TO PROBLEM SOLVE

We all start off with an inherent self-worth, attested to by looking on any infant's face. As life unfolds, we want to build on what we have, our values, and our accomplishments. Sometimes, though, we become complacent and defensive. It is more comfortable to just do things the familiar way, the way our parents did. This is done out of habit, without examining the effect of such habits.

We develop by valuing and acknowledging what we have received from those who raised us. Yet assimilating those experiences also requires balancing and redressing. It begs the question: Which part of our parents' and family's influence was misleading, ineffective, and damaging?

The troubles we experienced as children can continue to make us fearful of change. Change becomes associated with uncertainty, reminding us of our past negative experiences. On the surface we may be experiencing conflict with our children, but where does this discomfort originate; what is its source?

We see the negative results, but sometimes choose to ignore the problems themselves. Yet some part of us knows that stirring things up is exactly what is needed to progress with our lives. This healthy inner voice tells us life's circumstances call to us for needed changes, but the old patterns still bind us. It reminds me of the book entitled *I Hate You, Please Don't Leave Me*.

OUR SEARCH FOR WHOLENESS

Examining problems from the past can lead to solutions in the present. In the short run, though, it may cause some discomfort. By dealing with the area in question, we go through it and find ways to release and heal.

On the other hand, when we resist examining what troubles us, we remain uneasy, possibly creating family conflict and addiction. Fortunately, there are many ways to get help, such as meditating, attending workshops, healing through artwork, writing in a journal, talking with trusted friends, and reading books like this one. Good counseling and therapy can be part of this journey, and such efforts to heal should be considered a resource, not a stigma.

In our search for wholeness, we need to realize that problem solving is for everyone, not just the problem child or the depressed adult. Ultimately, we come to recognize that problems are normal—and covering up problems just creates more problems and keeps us stuck. In other words, our kids don't have to be permanent members of the detention hall to recognize that improvement is in order. And our own life doesn't have to be in a shambles for us to know things need to be addressed so we can truly move on.

Everyday stress and underlying confusion constitute feedback calling on us to face our challenges, encouraging us to improve our lives. Dealing with problems unlocks the riddles of our past. The past carries into our present and our future; it can be a strengthening or weakening influence, depending on our relationship to it.

Life's disharmony helps us by sending a message: It is in everyone's interest to create more understanding and to find solutions.

Fortunately, there are many ways to improve communication, some of which I will offer in this book. Helping children with their development holds some of our greatest lessons in life, which also opens us up to great joy and freedom. Life is a journey of self-discovery, changing and unfolding from moment to moment. The people around us are mirrors, showing us what is working and what is not.

As our ability to communicate improves, we are of greater help to ourselves and to those in our lives. And as the next chapter discusses, improving our awareness and our skills puts our life more in balance.

CHAPTER TWO

Finding the Balance

Here is an interesting exercise I learned from a chiropractor. With eyes closed, stretch your neck from side to side several times. End the exercise by placing your head in what you sense is a balanced, middle position, and then open your eyes. If you look in a mirror at where your head ends up, you might be surprised to find it is not centered; instead you may find your head tilted in an off-center position.

Similar to the experience of the head-and-neck exercise, we are continually shifting positions in life, sometimes ending up off-center without realizing it. In each moment of our lives, we go toward balance or away from it. When we are in balance, harmony occurs between our body, mind, emotions, and spirit.

In order to live a more balanced life, we need to address our "imbalances." On the one hand, we certainly don't want to obsess on our imbalances. On the other hand, we don't want to deny our problems, ignoring the real effect they have on us.

The "balance" comes from dealing with issues as they arise, using the ongoing feedback of our daily existence. These are the clues that are internally and externally being sent to us so we can grow and connect with ourselves—and, in turn, help others such as our children.

When we address our imbalances, we also clear the way for children to find their balance as they grow through different stages. Here are some areas affecting our balance and the chapters in the book that address them:

- **Beliefs:** Are they healthy or unhealthy? Do we see ourselves as empowered and lovable, or do we consider ourselves as helpless victims, at odds with others? (Chapters 4, 5, 7, 10, 11, 13, 17)

- **Trust:** Are we too trusting (naïve) or not trusting enough (cynical)? (Chapter 4)

- **Listening:** How well do we listen to children, and how well do they listen to us? (Chapter 6)

- **Feelings:** Are we able to appropriately express emotions? (Chapter 7)

- **Anger:** Can we let anger help us get our needs and desires met? Or does it become a defense mechanism, keeping others at a distance, masking underlying feelings and distorted thinking? (Chapter 8)

- **Boundaries:** Are we striking the balance between being too rigid and too loose? (Chapter 9)

- **Remorse:** Are we appropriately embarrassed and regretful or do we beat ourselves up with shame-based condemnation? Can we help children develop healthy remorse? (Chapters 11, 12)

- **Honesty:** How well do we encourage kids to be honest, even when they misbehave? During those troubling experiences, can we appropriately address their misbehavior while giving them recognition for telling the truth? And how honest are we? (Chapter 13)

- **Courage:** Can we discriminate between courage and destructive risk-taking? (Chapter 14)

- **Supervision of Children:** Are we being consistent, avoiding being negligent or overprotective? We want kids to gain independence as they mature, while we still maintain safety and security. This includes appropriate consequences and interventions. (Chapter 15)

- **Consistency:** Can we structure the environment for stability without becoming rigid? (Chapter 16)

You can evaluate the above areas for yourself and the kids in your life. Consider which areas are mostly in balance and which are mostly out of balance. The patterns you recognize in yourself relate to those you are seeing in children. For further insight, consider how balanced your caregivers were in each area.

TAKING APPROPRIATE ACTION

Life is a series of adjustments. We can either proactively address areas of imbalance, or wait until they become so out of whack that they hit us in the form of illness or conflict.

Also, take heart. Instead of assigning any blame to ourselves, which only adds to the problem, realize that through the examination process we are strengthening ourselves—on the road to recovery and wholeness.

By recognizing our strengths and weaknesses, we take appropriate action. This is part of our journey to heal and grow in our personal fulfillment, a path for ourselves and our kids. Even though children are on their own unique journey, their paths intersect ours when they are within our care.

Developing our ability to communicate is a lifelong process. It comes out of our experience, observations, and studies. This book can prompt you to gain new insights, skills, and approaches to better communicate and resolve family troubles. In the process, you will become more aware of yourself, becoming more self-reflective and better balanced. This will transfer to those around you; in particular, you can have a greater positive impact on children's development and their ability to communicate in healthy and creative ways.

To get an overview of how to help children, let's look at the stages of their development.

CHAPTER THREE

Mapping Your Course

Now that you have begun examining and resolving more of your own issues, it is time to see where we are going on this journey of getting through to kids, which includes getting through to yourself. As you navigate through the sometimes-rocky waters of your blockages, you can also help direct the children in your life through their difficulties.

Although there are common stages in every child's growth, each person's journey is unique, transcending an exact pattern. Use developmental stages as a reference. But consider every situation as a new event that has something to teach you in the moment—offering insights about the child and about yourself.

This chapter contains an overview of childhood development stages; it concludes with a description of how growing up is a part of our spiritual journey.

KNOWING CHILDHOOD DEVELOPMENT STAGES

It is helpful to identify the stages of children's development, to give us some reference points on where we started and where we are going. There are different descriptions of this progression, so I will offer one version. Realize that all the stages interrelate as well as build on one another. If a child is deficient in one area, other aspects of his or her life will be affected as well.

And of course adult deficiencies often stem from incomplete development during childhood. As you read these stages, ask which areas you feel are strong and weak in your own development. Know that we all have received setbacks at various stages of childhood. Those areas become sensitive, surrounded by defenses to protect our vulnerabilities. Those past hurts that we still carry with us are the "buttons" kids know how to locate and push.

You can use this book and your own resources to examine those stunted areas, to help heal yourself as you help heal the children in your life.

> *Liberation comes by changing automatic reactions to intentional responses.*

Responding means using our understanding to make a conscious choice; whereas reactions are automatic and unthinking. When we respond to kids, they become empowered, and so do we.

To progress, the first step is to recognize weaknesses and strengths. By finding out where you are strong, you know what to reinforce; by finding out where you are weak, you know what to change. For example, if you are easily frustrated when others—adults as well as kids—oppose your opinions, you might reexamine relevant childhood stages, such as toddler and teenage experiences.

- **Infancy (0 to 9-18 months):** Involves basic issues of trust, since infants' physical and emotional needs are dependent on the caregiver(s). Feelings of safety and closeness play a prominent role.

- **Toddler (9-18 months to 3 years):** Toddlers explore the immediate environment. With the help of their caregivers, they learn what is safe to explore and where boundaries begin and end. Children can gather a sense of their own feelings and thoughts. They can separate from caregivers while still being loved by them.

- **Pre-School Child (3 to 6 years):** Children explore beginning competencies and deal with success and failure, interacting with other children. They learn more how to share and empathize. Children learn that behaviors have consequences, and that fantasy differs from reality.

- **Grade-School Child (6 to 12 years):** Children's development grows more outside the family as the social world of peers comes more into play. How they fit into this broader world of school and relationships is a key to their development. Youngsters develop more internal controls, determining what is their responsibility, collaborating and competing with others.

- **Teenager (13 to 19 years):** Teenagers transit between childhood and adulthood. Their independence entails further separating from their family. As teenagers seek to develop their own identity and values, their self-esteem can significantly drop compared to earlier periods. Peers replace family as the group teens turn to for support, so fitting in becomes increasingly important. Issues of emotional and sexual intimacy emerge. Teens grow quite concerned with their body images. They become absorbed with self-discovery in the larger world of school and society. As teens mature, their self-esteem often improves.

You, the reader, are probably in your adulthood stage, although at times you may wonder. To successfully experience your life now, you can use what you have mastered from childhood. You can also continue to progress by healing the wounds from childhood as best you can. Remember, this is not a competition or quest for perfection.

In order to progress through childhood, we need to know the common imbalances that occur. As discussed in Harville Hendrix's writings, we tend to "minimize" or "maximize" parts of certain stages, depending on how we were raised. Minimizing means creating a pattern of lacking healthy care; maximizing means a pattern of excessive or invasive care. At any stage, there may be a weak link in the developmental pattern. To give an example: As a toddler, the child may have little parental guidance for reliable, healthy boundaries (minimized); or the young person may have been overly protected (maximized).

Since we all have been raised in an imperfect world, there will be areas in our life that can use some healing. Wherever we have been wounded in our own development, it will show up in our relationships with children. That's why they know how to push our "buttons." We unconsciously protect those deficiencies by defenses and rationalizations. Our compensations then appear to kids as inconsistent and insincere behavior, the very material that ignites conflict between adults and children. Our "buttons" connect to the vulnerable, unfulfilled parts of our own childhood. As we work on our own issues, examining where we floundered through childhood, we grow within, providing us the strength and know-how to effectively help kids.

We can work on our own issues through discussions with peers, mates, and counselors. We can also become involved in journaling, artwork, prayer and meditation, and relevant classes that can be important for our own development as well as for children's.

SPIRITUAL DEVELOPMENT

The previous childhood development stages don't account for soul development, or, for that matter, the existence of the soul itself. To put things in perspective, remember that "soul" is just one of many words describing inner wisdom and connection to our source and unity.

Spiritual development is integral to being human. My understanding is that the soul would seem to be a part of us that transcends our bodies and even our whole life, something that exists beyond and through time. Our physical, emotional, and mental development reflects our spirit, the greater aspect of ourselves that permeates all of our existence. Our spiritual evolution is the backdrop for all stages of development. I believe that it helps account for children's different understanding and awareness. Two children can have similar upbringings and respond quite differently to the same experiences. These experiences present lessons a child is in this life to learn, and how the young person responds to them has important consequences for spiritual development.

To understand this more metaphysical viewpoint, imagine a soul before it inhabits a physical body. That soul has its objectives and interests for spiritual fulfillment. It then finds ways to meet its needs, intent on gathering the experience and knowledge for its progress.

> *Some of our most difficult human experiences can be necessary and beneficial for our spiritual development.*

Life's highs and lows, the beauty and the heartache, inform and develop the soul.

In each stage of childhood development, the individual strives to be a part of a larger sphere, spiraling upward to connect with a bigger world. Infants, who are constantly monitored by caregivers, relate to the world through the perceptions of their caregivers. Next, toddlers interact with their immediate environment. Pre-schoolers want an identity separate from others, exploring different roles by role playing. Grade-schoolers test their mettle with peers, finding themselves mirrored by other children. By adolescence, teenagers want more intimacy, to know themselves on another level through experimentation and close relationships outside the family.

All of this fans out into adulthood, with its concerns about jobs, marriage, and families. After children grow up, they seek a place in the community, and ultimately in the world. They carry with them all the losses, and all the gains, from childhood.

The Bowl of Light

We can understand more about our opportunities to grow by examining the traditional Hawaiians' culture. These traditional people believe that each person comes into life with a bowl of light that illuminates our journey for a lifetime. Hawaiian Huna psychology teaches that as we connect with our inner bowl of light, we understand more of our true nature and who we are meant to be. This inner light then shines forth as we share it with others. To guide people along their spiritual path, the Hawaiians also have a Golden Rule that translates to: "Whatever I do to you, I do to myself."

Paradoxically, the more we can help youth realize their uniqueness, the more they can connect with others.

The more children can see themselves in the faces and hearts of others, the more they realize their connection with everything, knowing that they travel a path that transcends understanding yet is somehow meant just for them.

The way I understand it, the soul watches, advises, learns with the child through each stage of his or her development. It witnesses the emotional ups and downs, the intellectual terrain, and the physical changes that mark each child's existence on Earth. The soul knows what the person has learned and what still needs to be resolved, so it can be mended into the fabric of its wholeness.

As we connect more with our own spiritual presence and see things from its perspective, we gather great humility and respect for life. Our bowl of light glows stronger. We hold even more dear our relationship with children as we help them with their journey, which is part of our own journey. That is why asking the child what she learns from an experience can be so valuable. Because who is doing the learning? The learner includes both the child and the future adult; and all parts are contained within the ever-present soul that continues to grow through all it encounters, unifying into an ever-greater wholeness.

Part 2

GETTING TO THE BASICS

"Where did I come from?" the baby asked its mother.
She answered, half-crying, half-laughing,
and clasping the baby to her breast:
"You were hidden in my heart as its desire, my darling.
You were in the dolls of all my childhood games.
In all my hopes and my loves, in my life,
in the life of my mother, and in her mother before her,
you have lived. In the lap of the Eternal Spirit
you have been nursed and anticipated for ages."

- RABINDRANATH TAGORE

CHAPTER FOUR

Building Trust

Dr. Ken Magid and Carole McKelney noted in *High Risk* that "children need to learn how to trust others before they can contribute to society. Teaching to count isn't nearly as important as teaching children what counts. We cannot call it education unless it also teaches children honesty, self-respect, and respect to others."

Trust has been defined as "a firm reliance on the integrity, ability, or character of a person or thing." Trust is a bridge between you and the child. To understand more about that bridge, think of people you trust. They are people who will listen to your thoughts and feelings without being judgmental. They are accepting of you and willing to speak their own mind. Although not perfect, trustworthy people are reliable; their words generally correspond to their actions.

To the extent that you embody the elements of trust yourself—such as respect, honesty, consistency, and good boundaries—you can then teach the child these qualities so he or she can earn your trust. Naturally, you may need to do some repair work on your own trustworthiness in order to solidly connect with the young person—and that can be discreetly shared with the child. "Yes, Johnny, I'm being more honest at work. I used to come to work late. Now I let people know when I'm late, and make up the time I missed." This candor and vulnerable sharing becomes a great teaching tool and will go a long way toward having the child trust you.

From children's early stages of development, look for clear ways you can build trust with them. Your experiences develop the bridge of trust between you and young people. Sometimes the structure weakens and collapses, needing re-building. Vital to school, work, and relationships, trust becomes a sacred connection to so much that is valuable in our lives.

THE TWO SIDES OF TRUST

To understand trust, realize that it has two aspects: You can demonstrate it by showing you are trustworthy and by trusting others. In other words, people can trust you, and you can select people to trust. To illustrate both elements, here are some examples that teenagers have shared with me.

1. **Trustworthiness.** Teens say they are trustworthy by controlling their tempers and impulses. They deserve trust for being persistent and keeping their promises. Such commitments include pursuing their goals, such as good grades and behavioral commitments to parents and teachers.

2. **Trusting others.** Teens cite how they have trusted others to keep their commitments to them. Teens have exhibited trust when they share their thoughts about personal matters such as

family deaths and tragedies to teachers and classmates. They have trusted others when they are vulnerable enough to ask others for assistance, such as in playing a game or using a computer program.

★ TOOL 3 ★
Establishing Trust

Here are several areas where you can teach children how to be trustworthy and trust others. As already mentioned, remember to use yourself as an example.

- **Acknowledge trustworthy behavior.** Let kids know their actions merit your trust. "Thanks for returning this. It helps me trust you."

- **Point out untrustworthy behavior.** Conversely, if children have taken something without permission, you can explain how their actions violate trust. Trust is earned over repeated honest, caring, and responsible actions. The next time they ask to borrow something, you can say, "I am counting on you to return this." Or "Can I trust you to be careful with that?" If children succeed, compliment them for their trustworthiness.

- **Determine "off trust" behavior.** If there is a repeated disregard for your trust, then the youngster may have to go on to a temporary off trust status. "Danny, I will take you to the store after you've shown me for a while that I can trust you. So this time, I can't take you. Let's see how trustworthy you are over the next few weeks around the house."

Find ways to work with children, not against them. You can set standards, while showing ways they can improve.

SECRETS AND TRUST

Evan Imber-Black writes in *The Secret Life of Families* that secrets help young children develop a sense of themselves. Through codes, clubs, and secret pacts, children learn how to carve out a private existence for themselves, separate from adults. They explore loyalties, boundaries, relationships, and how lying and honesty affect family and friends. Healthy secrets can teach the child lessons in profound ways.

However, when children feel ashamed of their thoughts, feelings, or behaviors, they may keep things hidden. This can reflect on how their caregivers have treated them. Caregivers put kids on the defensive when they have too high expectations of them and when they are too controlling of them. In addition, children may consider the adults who supervise them unable to deal with their secrets, so they feel unsupported and keep things hidden.

Having secrets can be an unhealthy practice for children when it serves to hide their misconduct from adults. Sometimes children feel they will be unfairly punished, so they want to avoid the pain. We need to make sure that we treat kids fairly, with compassion and understanding. We also need to follow through on the consequences resulting from misbehavior and deceit. Thank children for their courage and responsibility when they discuss problems.

It is healthy to acknowledge children for sharing secrets that hide serious problems. Yet it may still be necessary to deal with the poor decisions and harmful behavior that have occurred. Chapter 15 explores how to give reasonable consequences for what they did. Perhaps children can help you determine an appropriate consequence. If a kid stole something, then he would have to pay it back and offer an apology. If she lied, then the youngster would need to explain why, including her feelings and thoughts. She would also discuss how her lie affected others' trust, actions, and feelings.

Respecting children after discovering they did something disrespectful is an act of love. Showing young people such respect builds trust.

Teenagers, like younger children, also have secrets in their quest for independence. Traditional societies transitioned kids into adulthood through rituals, which often included secret-keeping. Our culture does not have those rites of passage, but teens do find ways to keep parts of their development and experimentation undisclosed to adults.

Teenagers now live in a world where alcohol and drugs, date rape, suicide, and violence abound. In relating to young people, it is important to consider the potential danger of a secret. Are we talking about an alcoholic drink consumed at a party, or an addiction to alcohol? Without moralizing, discuss the dangers of behavior. Use your listening skills. The doors for communication need to be open in a world where police estimate 60 percent of teens don't tell their parents when they are mugged in shopping malls or on city streets. Toxic secrets hide dangerous behavior and experiences. Find ways to explore with kids where secrets cover areas that could harm them.

It is also important to distinguish dangerous secrets from privacy. Privacy becomes an ever-increasing factor in a child's development toward individuation. Granting children sufficient privacy expands as the child matures; and how adults offer children privacy can be the difference between healthy boundaries and shaming intrusions. Violating children's needs for privacy can drive them to secretive behavior. Allowing children privacy provides them a sense of modesty and develops their selfhood. Take time to evaluate children's increasing needs for privacy and how well you honor that part in their development.

Also, be mindful that a person's need for privacy differs from maintaining a dangerous secret. Such secret-keeping breeds hiding and concealment. Also in contrast to privacy, unhealthy secrets isolate us, distancing us from the very resources we need to heal and problem-solve.

TRUST DURING ADOLESCENCE

Part of learning to trust involves learning *whom* to trust. By the time kids reach adolescence, there can be fierce loyalties among peers. Like threatening thunderclouds, intimidating fears of being a "snitch" hover over teens, no matter how justified it might be to report on a peer's misconduct. In terms of childhood development, connecting with peers does help a young person develop independence and mature into adulthood. The complexity comes as the black-and-white morality of childhood blends into the grayer morality of adolescence, where experimentation and peer loyalty can result in poor decisions and irresponsible behavior.

If you have established trust with children when they are younger, they are more likely to maintain that connection as they mature into adolescence. Even if there has been difficulty fostering trust, you can still find helpful resources. There are many ways to show young people about what Shakespeare meant when he said, "To thine own self be true."

It becomes important to explore with children how associating with untrustworthy people is not genuine friendship if the relationship is based on hurting and taking advantage of others.

Discussions about trust need to be more in a form of gentle questions than a lecture. Here are sample questions: "What has she done to earn your trust?" "What have you done to earn trust?" "Does it help keeping certain things a secret?" "How will it help you?" "How will it hurt you?" This can be offered with heartfelt concern, rather than as an interrogation.

Help kids be accountable and learn from their mistakes. They must get the idea that you still accept them, however serious their transgressions. Praise children for their honesty and help them see how actions have consequences and good boundaries prevent problems.

TRUST: BREAKING THE CYCLE OF ABUSE

Abuse, including physical, verbal, and sexual abuse, destroys trust. The dictionary offers three definitions of abuse: "harmful treatment; unkind, cruel, or rude words; wrong use." Unfortunately, we live in a world where abusing kids is an all-too-common occurrence with a long history behind it. To address such serious difficulties, abused children and adults may need professional help. Even if you do not deal directly with those who have suffered from abusive backgrounds, it is still helpful to expand your awareness to gain insight and compassion.

Having dealt with emotionally disturbed children for many years in the classroom, I noticed that the foundation for kids' progress lies in trusting others who can help them.

> *Having others to trust is a fundamental building block in life, and it leads to learning how to trust oneself.*

To help us better understand trust, we can study kids who thrive in spite of abusive upbringings. They have been called "resilient" children.

Those who have become resilient have found an older person to trust and help guide them. But of course it is difficult for wounded children to risk trusting another when their previous caregivers did not develop a relationship based on trust. They are apt to wonder why they should trust you after suffering deep disappointment from those they were supposed to have trusted. And there is an element of risk and self-disclosure in trust. To become resilient, young people need to share thoughts and feelings.

We need to make it clear to children that we can help—we are trustworthy. Perhaps most important, kids need to develop trust for their own welfare and to break the cycle of abuse that can continue without help. Because what happens when abused children face stress? How will they react? They tend to withdraw or hurt others, especially by the time they become adults with kids in their own adult lives.

A speaker, Bill, shared this story about when he was growing up in the 1950s.

One day Bill and his father looked out their living-room window and saw the neighboring twelve-year-old, Tommy, being dragged across the lawn by his father. The father pulled the boy by his ear. Young Bill's father looked down at his son and commented, "Boy, Tommy is in trouble now! He's going to get what's coming to him." Young Bill felt a wave of fear ripple through him. He breathed a sigh of relief that he was not in Tommy's shoes that day.

Tommy eventually became an adult and maybe a father. This poses a question: How do you think he would treat his kids? For that matter, one wonders how Bill treated his children since his father condoned such abusive "ear-pulling" behavior.

Once children have become wounded from abuse, they can be naturally defensive. They try to protect themselves from others and put on a tough exterior. On a purely survival level, this may prevent others from hurting them. But they may participate in hurting others as an unconscious way to deal with their anger and rage from earlier mistreatment.

In my class, I sometimes see emotionally wounded children act as if they are bleeding while at the same time refusing treatment. And with emotional wounds there is no physical bleeding, but the evidence comes out in their thoughts, feelings, and behavior. They say they don't need help, implicitly knowing there will be discomfort when treating the wound. At first, kids may be too sensitive, too defensive to directly address their hurt. Trust and healing take time. By neglecting those inner wounds, the problems persist, and young people can easily victimize others much as they were victimized themselves.

Children will still act out their inner pain by disturbing others until they are sufficiently healed and at peace with themselves. Such disturbances call for the adult to separate kids from their actions, realizing that the youngster's underlying wounds can cause harm to themselves and others. In other words, you can accept troubled children while not accepting the trouble they cause.

Children's inappropriate behavior reflects the hurt they feel from inside.

To support kids, make your sincerity and guidance clear to them by your words and actions. You are offering children help, and it is their choice whether they accept it or not. If they refuse help, explore the consequences with them in a clear and nonjudgmental way. Do they want to hurt others like they were hurt? Talking about their concerns can go a long way in the healing process. Wounded children, and adults, are disconnected from their feelings and those of others. Shame and self-protection cause them to hide their wounds. Consider also whether professional help is needed.

The abuse cycle perpetuates itself unless wounded children find a way to transcend the pattern. The way to escape is for them to trust someone who can listen to their thoughts and feelings. Contained in children's minds and hearts are the pain and shame that weigh them down. By accepting children, you encourage them to trust enough to share their pain so they can heal. Just remember to allow time for the relationship to develop. As a deep wound takes time to heal, it also takes time to establish trust with children who have experienced an abusive past.

THE POSITIVE PATH

Children know a brighter future when they learn how to trust. To assist them in understanding their possibilities, I sometimes describe two paths for kids. One is called the path of destruction, or as one student referred to it, "the crazy path." The other one is the path of life, or as another student called it, "the path of freedom." Kids who learn how to trust are better able to follow the positive path, and you can help them stay on it.

As an adult, you can show young people you are human and make mistakes, and perhaps at times have strayed onto the destructive path yourself. Yet still convey to them that you care and are reliable. Children succeed when they realize they can trust others, and that others have experienced difficulties in developing trust, too.

You can take time to track your own trustworthiness and look for ways to bolster this crucial area of human development. Tools in this book can be a resource for you.

MAINTAINING AND DEVELOPING TRUST

You are already developing trust. Keep on trusting! Here is a list to help you and your child trust yourself and others:

- Keep pointing out ways you trust the child: "I trust you to go by yourself."

- Keep sharing your own thoughts and feelings: "I sometimes have trouble accepting rules too. But I know that if I do accept them, I can get things I want, and people will trust me. That makes me feel satisfied and happy."

- Keep maintaining appropriate boundaries: "Carol, when you stand that close to me it makes me uncomfortable. I like being around you, but it would be good to keep a little more distance between us."

- Keep finding out what the child thinks and believes: "It sounds like you really get angry when you have to do something you don't like. It can be difficult not getting your way."

- Keep talking about the positive and negative consequences of behavior. Without preaching, explore the kinds of actions that result from those thoughts and beliefs: "What will happen if you keep making fun of your peers?" "Will they be able to trust you?" "Do you want that?"

- Keep having the child find alternatives with your help: "So you think sharing your CDs with him might work."

- Keep following up on healthy alternatives: "I like the way you shared your things with him. "

- Keep evaluating the child's actions in terms of how it helps or hurts her and others: "Would it hurt yourself or hurt others if you cheated on the test?"

- Keep yourself free of judging the child, accepting the young person while still having him or her be accountable. "I still care for you. Let's figure out how we can improve the situation."

- Keep evaluating yourself and the child in terms of trust. Do your words, actions, and body language promote trust? "When you do your chores, even though you don't like it, it helps me trust you. You also used a nice tone of voice when we talked about it."

Continue this conscious work of developing trust, bridging any troubles and allowing relationships a way to grow. Trust is a powerful connector between people of all ages. It starts with building trust in ourselves, and then we can reach kids so they can build their own bridge of trust to us and others in their lives.

To continue our relationships with kids, let's look at what to do when communication breaks down, and children are unwilling to share their agitated thoughts and feelings with us.

CHAPTER FIVE

Breaking the Ice

What about when the child is unwilling to talk about problems? I often receive this question when I talk with groups. It has to do with getting stuck...and unstuck.

★ TOOL 4 ★
Jump Starting the Discussion Checklist

When children are unwilling or unable to discuss what troubles them, you can use this checklist to help them through difficult times:

✓ **First, look at who has the problem.** Is the problem the child's, yours or both? Ownership is a key. Who exactly is responsible for what? If the child broke a dish, he needs to take some responsibility, since the item belongs to his family. If he broke your personal item, he needs fuller responsibility for damaging another's belonging. If he broke his own toy or possession, well, he may have to just live without it...for a while at least. Maybe earning back what he ruined would help. In responding to the situation, bear in mind that sometimes the young person is unaware of the problem he creates, such as making noise when another person is concentrating. Perhaps the problem is more over your reaction to the child. Ask yourself if you are being overly critical or too lax. If such an adjustment is needed, then it's time to go within and see how you can change to help improve the external situation.

✓ **Here is an interesting question to ask yourself: When do you sense your own resistance to dealing with a problem that involves the youngster?** What are your feelings, thoughts, beliefs, and behaviors? Are any of these reflected in the resistant child you are now trying to help? One ten-year-old girl told me she was very resentful about having to clean her room before going out to play, since her parents' bedroom was generally left so messy.

✓ **Once you establish who owns the problem, then timing comes into play.** Forcing a child to talk when he is not ready may aggravate the problem and cause more resistance. Find a time when the child is not defensive and is more relaxed. You may want to tell the child directly that you know it's not a good time to talk now, but you want to talk at an appointed time.

✓ **Movement and engaging activities naturally remove a child's resistance and defense mechanisms.** It can be easier to talk with a child during a game, a sport, or a walk.

✓ **Once the time is right, you can begin with an obvious and innocuous statement, such as "It looks like you have been sitting there a while."** These truisms, obvious statements, create rapport and agreement in the child.

✓ **If you do start a discussion and it breaks down, it may be time to examine yourself again.** Where do you get stuck in the dialogue? Note what is going on at that point. Check your own emotional state. Look at the overall pattern of how you respond when the child is resistant to discussion. Ask yourself:

- How ready am I to listen to the child's problems with an open mind and without interrupting?

- How composed am I?

- If I want the child to work things out, how flexible and reasonable am I?

✓ **Besides finding the right time to talk with the young person, be willing to share your concerns and feelings.** Children are usually open when you are. Be vulnerable and share your fears, frustrations, and anxieties in an honest, forthright way. Remember your intent is to share your feelings, not dump them. Be sensitive to the child's needs. "I'm concerned, Mary, that you might hurt something. You seem upset, and that worries me. I know something is bothering you, and I care for you. I'd really appreciate hearing from you. What's going on?" In contrast to a lecturing or advice-giving style, this kind of sharing is one area where adults could do more of the talking with kids.

Your heartfelt sincerity will be heard. Children will be more disposed to open up, and when they do, just be sure to listen. This is no time to play the expert know-it-all. Be quick to listen and slow to give advice and consequences. Ownership of problems comes into play. If children are affecting your responsibilities and needs, then share that fact, inviting solutions that both of you can honor. If the issue concerns your transporting the child to the mall, for instance, you can explain to the child about scheduling considerations that you have. You can point out how you must balance other parts of your life along with helping the child meet his or her needs.

You may need to establish some limits and boundaries to help the young person set standards. "We need to work out how often I can take you to places you want to go. Let's make a schedule and see if there are other ways you can get to where you want to go."

Breaking through a child's isolation develops trust and security. Feeling more comfortable, the child is far more likely to discuss problems with you in the future. Your confidence, self-esteem, and self-knowledge will grow as well.

Now that the child is willing to talk with you, let's look at how you can be a good listener.

CHAPTER SIX

Learning to Listen

"She doesn't hear a word I say!" "He totally tunes me out." "Kids just don't listen." These common complaints by adults bring up the question: How did kids acquire these poor listening skills? This in turn leads us to ask how well do we listen to children?

To find some answers, let's consider these questions. How well did your parents listen to you? How sensitive were they to you? Did they spend time effectively helping you when problems arose? Or, alternatively, when they were available, did they tend to do most of the talking and little of the listening?

Adults tend to dominate children. Such a heavy-handed approach includes excessive explaining and telling children what to do. A powerful belief system still exists : Children are to be seen and not heard.

We are supposed to be the models and mentors for kids, authorities they trust and respect. The trouble is we often don't know how to be the authority, and we can end up being the authoritarian. Today, we know an authoritarian approach, which dominates and belittles, is counterproductive. But, like actions reflecting racial prejudice, the authoritarian response still prevails in many situations. Becoming a genuine authority calls on us to develop certain abilities, one of which is listening.

Talking is easier than listening. An effective communicator, though, needs to listen as well as to speak.

Listening includes tuning in to our own thoughts and words, as well as those of others. By self-reflection, and by noticing others' responses to our words, we have continual feedback on how effectively we communicate.

In childhood development, infants listen before learning to speak. This is nature's cue to help young ones notice their surroundings. Yet somehow this natural development gets lost. The ancient Roman sage Epictetus noted that people have two ears and one mouth so we can listen twice as much as we speak. Our society has forgotten this message, as it's drowned out in all sorts of noise: commercials, loud music, and habitual talking. The quiet is often lost. In that quiet, we learn to listen, just as we once did as a fetus inside a womb.

As a teacher, I have dealt with many social workers, counselors, and educators. From my observations, these professions often produce big talkers; I was one of them. To balance my ability to communicate, I had to consciously work on my listening skills. Too many times I heard the response, "You didn't hear what I said."

When you talk a lot, you can convince yourself of just about anything. But when you listen, you can find out what's really going on. When you talk to kids *after* careful listening, you are more informed and aware. Then your words mean more and kids naturally listen to you.

There was a revealing 1998 *USA Weekend Report on Teens and Self Image* that asked the question, "Do you think adults generally value your opinion?" Over one-third of grade 6-12 respondents said adults don't value their opinions. The report also noted that parents were by far the most important influence in the students' lives. This study indicates that too many children believe we are not listening. They can then become what has been jokingly called "daddy- or mommy-deaf."

Let's look closer at listening to children. Parenthetically, listening to children also helps you listen to adults.

THREE KEYS TO BETTER LISTENING

1. Use active listening. One of the basic listening habits to develop goes by various names such as mirroring, reflective listening, or active listening. I will use the term "active listening" for the sake of this discussion. Like all listening skills, active listening revolves around concentrating on what is being said. It often includes repeating back to the other person what she has said. This may be a summary or word-for-word description of what you heard, letting the listener know she has been heard. Simply put, you carefully hear what the speaker says and feed back to her what has been said.

Active listening also involves direct eye contact with the listener. Other nonverbal behavior can include using acknowledging sounds and head nods to convey that you are listening.

Although active listening can easily be learned by adults and children, it takes effort, especially at first, to put into practice. It calls for you to put your mind on hold—suspending your own thoughts—as the other person speaks. This shows respect for the speaker and helps you develop an open mind to what is being said. Such intentional listening also lets you be in the moment, truly experiencing the communication that presents itself. It lets you live your life, experiencing what someone is trying to convey to you, instead of following the script from your own mind, an agenda that removes you from the actual experience of listening to the child.

And if we don't listen to kids, why should they listen to us? Listening to us because of our age is not a very satisfying reason; it is more a justification that we are entitled to have kids listen to us because we are older and usually bigger. We need to demonstrate that we have learned from our years of experience by truly listening to what children say to us. If we interrupt them and dominate the discussion, we are rearing another generation of poor listeners, who will pass on an unwanted legacy to the next generation.

2. Validate the speaker's thoughts. Therapists Harville Hendrix and Helen Hunt did some impressive research for their book *Giving the Love That Heals*. In working with couples and parents, they concluded that active listening by itself could be ineffective. You can listen to a person's words and still use them as ammunition against the person to prove your point. When speaking to a youngster, you can repeat the child's words and then summarily dismiss what he said, which translates to the child as a dismissal of his own worth. Such disrespect undermines relationships. To be a good listener, then, entails more than just reciting back what the child has said.

Hendrix and Hunt found two other ingredients in addition to active listening that were needed for good listening. One of the listening skills was validating. This includes accepting children's thinking without necessarily agreeing with it. Youngsters' words hold their own validity for them, regardless of how distorted the thinking. They are valid on some level, perhaps in ways we have not recognized ourselves. Rather than trying to reject kids' thoughts, our validation offers respect for their thinking. And don't we want people to respect our thoughts, however different or wrong-headed they may turn out to be?

Validating allows you to see a point of view different from your own. You want to create rapport with the youngster, which provides a feeling of exchange when you communicate. It promotes ways to give and receive, rather than ways to attack and defeat. A climate of exchange and respect validates everyone.

Here is what happened one time when I spoke to a small group about listening.

The group was composed of adults and one ten-year-old girl, who was just there because she had accompanied her mother. Throughout the talk, she was absorbed by reading a book. At the end of the discussion, I complimented the adults for their successful listening. Suddenly, the young girl looked up from reading her book. She turned to her Mother in the next seat and said, "You don't listen to me!" Her mother, along with the rest of us, was taken aback. "What do you mean I don't listen to you? I hear what you say." The girl responded, "But you don't say anything back to me when I talk to you."

In other words, the mother actively listened to her daughter, but didn't *validate* her daughter's words. The mother needed to use validating phrases and appropriate body language (such as head nodding) to convey that she had listened.

Steven Spielberg referred to the validation he received during childhood when the American Film Institute honored him. The renowned film director's acceptance speech included credit to his parents when he said, "Thanks for giving me the opportunity to answer some of my own questions." His parents allowed him to find answers, rather than providing all the thinking, a process that validated Spielberg's questions and curiosity. In addition to recognizing kids' thoughts, we learn from Steve Spielberg another aspect of validation: listening to children's questions and letting them find the answers.

★ TOOL 5 ★
Phrasing For Validation

Here are some phrases to remember for validating a child's words:

- I can understand that.
- It makes sense.
- It's important for you.
- You have a point there.

Consider using one or more of these phrases, or something comparable, in your next meeting with the kids in your life. To get started, I will give a series of examples, and then you can follow by finding your own examples. I call this a "My Turn, Your Turn Sequence":

- "I can understand that you want to stay out that late with your friends."
  Now it's your turn: "I can understand that..."

- "It makes sense that you would want to buy that dress."
  Your turn: "It makes sense that..."
- "It's important for you to have that computer game."
  Your turn: "It's important for you..."
- "You have a point about my taking you to the mall."
  Your turn: "You have a point..."

As you validate children's thoughts, you support them regardless of how their thoughts compare with yours. You may disagree with their ideas and opinions, but children have a right to their thinking.

To develop their thinking ability,
which is crucial for self-development,
children need to be heard.

This requires validation through listening. By validating what young people say, you also teach them to be good listeners.

3. Empathize with the speaker's feelings. In addition to active listening and validating, Hendrix and Hunt complete the triad of good listening skills with empathizing. The dictionary defines empathy as "the power of imagining oneself to be another person, and so of sharing his/her feelings." Just as validating says a kid's thoughts are okay, empathizing says his or her feelings are acceptable.

Although feeling words are helpful, emotions can transcend verbal language. Children's words offer indications about their inner world, a world that is largely unconscious. Our own intuition can relate to youngsters' hidden worlds, not by analyzing, but by sensitizing ourselves to their feelings.

Emotions powerfully connect us to others. Be sure you get in touch with your own feelings, as children convey how they feel. However strange or frightening the feelings, children gain security when an adult identifies those feelings. You then acknowledge that children are not alone in those feelings, that adults experience them too. (Such discussions may help you see how your own feelings relate to those the child experiences.)

Empathizing with children helps them develop friendships and intimate relationships as they mature. Empathy also helps us bond with kids. We may notice closeness in subtle ways, such as how we feel around children and how they listen to us. On the other hand, when empathy is lacking, conflict and argument rule the day. Children need to learn how to manage the sways of their emotional states. By setting the example of listening to children's troubles, you pave a way for them to soothe and regulate themselves.

★ TOOL 6 ★
Phrasing For Empathy

Here are some phrases to help you with empathy:

- It looks [or sounds] like you feel...
- I can sense that you feel...
- I can imagine that you are experiencing...

To further help you empathize, here is another My Turn, Your Turn sequence, like we did in the previous section on validating. I provide the first example; you complete the following one.

- "It looks like you feel angry from the expression on your face."
  "It looks like you feel…"

- "I can sense that you feel lonely about not being invited to the party."
  "I can sense that you feel…"

- "I can imagine that you feel frustrated that your brother follows you around."
  "I can imagine that you…"

A note: Avoid using the phrase "I understand" or "I understand you." (This differs from the validating phrase "I understand that…" which connects with a specific part of the child's experience.) Such statements can elicit a disruptive, rather than soothing, response from the other person. For example, when a child is angry, the response of "I understand" might draw opposition. It can sound arrogant or insincere, denying the child's unique experience.

To review, here are the three keys to listening that we have discussed:

1. Use active listening.
2. Validate the speaker's thoughts.
3. Empathize with the speaker's feelings.

SELF-DISCLOSURE

Sometimes you can naturally follow up empathy with your own disclosures. Disclosing means taking a risk, that is, sharing your own intimate feelings and experiences with kids. The reward of appropriate disclosure, however, far outweighs the risk. By sharing that you too have troublesome feelings and experiences, you help kids realize your humanity. Children then realize that you grow from your challenges, and you also grow from disclosing them appropriately. Then you, and in turn your children, can use challenges as an opportunity to learn rather than a reason to complain and suffer.

Of course, disclosure should be used with discrimination. Misusing disclosure could lead to poor boundaries, letting dominating and excessive talking take over. Indiscriminate disclosure could impose a caretaking role on children, which is not their role.

The question to answer before disclosing is "Will my personal sharing help kids in what they are now going through?" If it will help them, then a heartfelt disclosure can be in order.

NOT GETTING MY WAY

"You didn't listen to me!" Have you ever heard those words from a young person in your life? They are often born out of frustration and anger. A child accusing you of not listening suggests at least two possibilities:

1. You neglected to actively listen, validate, empathize, and disclose sufficiently.

2. The youngster is operating from a limiting belief system about "not getting my way."

We have already dealt with the first possibility concerning the listening-skill components. The second situation of "you didn't listen to me" is different. In this case, you have attentively listened to the child, enough to be able to fully summarize what has been said. So the problem does not stem from your poor listening skills; instead, the conflict revolves around the child's wanting to get his or her way. Let's look closer at the child's limiting belief of "not getting my way."

Underlying feelings and thoughts are beliefs. A prevalent belief is that we should get what we want. From infancy, life is a series of experiences concerning what we can and cannot control. As children's worlds grow, so too do their attempts at independence, which include developing will and boundaries. Children may not be mature enough to reconcile their thoughts and feelings with the disappointments they experience. Their frustrated cries of "You don't listen to me" may make you confused and possibly defensive.

When children accuse you of not listening to their demands, you may have already actively listened and paraphrased what they said...to no avail. The kids just can't understand why you won't agree with what to them seems so important, necessary, and reasonable. They want to get their way! So children think, "You *couldn't* have heard me and still said 'no' to my request."

Delayed gratification may be a foreign concept at this point. Youth must face growing up into an ever-expanding world, a world where responsibility is balanced with privileges. As children seek maturity, they continue to test limits and boundaries, at once yearning for growth while at the same time resisting it. Frustration and tantrums can occur in the process.

By listening to their thoughts and feelings, you can help children see how their faulty belief—"I never get what I want"—traps them. You can also help them place healthy limits on their desires. Through your reasoning, questioning, and listening, most children will see that they *sometimes* get their way. "I sometimes get what I want" or "I can live without it" become enhancing beliefs that lead to growth and positive feelings. You also have your own values and budget that further define what the child can receive or earn.

For more help on this kind of processing, you might want to see my earlier book, *Getting Thru to Kids: Problem Solving with Children Ages 6 to 18,* which details a five-step process for transforming belief systems by working with feelings, thoughts and beliefs.

MOTIVATING YOURSELF TO LISTEN MORE

Being human, for both children and adults, is about growth and transformation; and developing listening skills figures in as a key component to our success. It is not a one-shot deal—as in "I've already done that [studied and improved listening]"—but a complex skill we develop throughout our lifetime.

Depending on your viewpoint, listening can be a tiresome task or an opportunity to connect with children.

Validating a child's thinking uses your brain; empathizing with a child uses your heart.

Effective listening becomes both active and passive, a basic process that powerfully combines doing with being. As children speak, you can think about what they say and also just be with them, allowing their words to flow through your attentive ears. As you listen with your mind and heart, children develop their minds and hearts as well. As a motivation for listening to kids, just remember the clarity and satisfaction you received when someone carefully listened to you. Listening helps everyone connect deeper with themselves, as well as with each other.

If we put enough value on listening, we will naturally find ways to improve, which will benefit ourselves and the kids around us. We can continue to study others who listen well, learn from those who listen poorly, read material on listening, and challenge ourselves to listen a little more today.

When we don't listen well to kids, communication falters. Then as we talk, children grow resistant to hearing our words. On the other hand, when we do listen to children, it provides a healing balm to their intense feelings and encouragement for their own thinking. Our attention offers kids a natural outlet to express what they are going through.

Listening to a child sends the message: You are someone. You are unique, distinct, and separate from me, with your own thoughts and feelings. I acknowledge you as a person, hear you out, and recognize your feelings and thoughts. Life becomes far richer when we know that we are not alone, and someone cares enough to listen to us.

This chapter noted that an essential part of listening involves paying attention to the speaker's feelings. The next chapter delves further into how crucial it is to know our own feelings as well as our children's.

CHAPTER SEVEN

Exploring Feelings

Feelings are ongoing throughout our lives, regardless of our age. Our emotional nature is an integral part of who we are. Feelings provide direct feedback to us. They help us successfully function and express ourselves. From the youngest to the oldest of us, we continually, moment-to-moment, experience different feelings.

Yet when I ask students who come into my class to write about or express feelings, they sometimes react by saying, "That's none of your business. It's private!" Although it's an understandable response, this defense blocks expressing feelings not only to others, but also to oneself. And it leads to further difficulties. It's curious that children may repeatedly "act out," that is, disturb others' boundaries and feelings. Yet the idea of finding out the source of their own troubles, which involves feelings, becomes somehow taboo and off limits. This avoidance of dealing with feelings can trigger a child's misbehaving around others. It sets up an environment where it is okay to avoid and repress negative feelings, but it is not okay to talk about those emotional triggers and what they mean.

Since feelings are an ongoing part of the human experience, and certainly a part of childhood development, shouldn't children become aware of this vital aspect of themselves?

Recognizing and dealing with feelings is a strength, not a weakness.

FOUR APPROACHES TO FEELINGS

What can we do with these ongoing feelings? How do we approach such a basic component of our existence? Here are four ways we deal with feelings:

1. **Deny feelings.** "I'm feeling nothing." Numbness and apathy are actual feelings (see the Feelings Inventory in the next chapter). When a person says he is feeling "nothing," it suggests that feelings are absent. Denying feelings cuts us off from our experiences, blocking the emotional feedback we are actually experiencing in the moment. Denying feelings does not make a person more objective. It might make him "cold" and "clinical," which are apathetic feelings. Numbing out indicates a blockage, for feelings are the key to our hearts. Without them we become heartless and confused.

2. **Dramatize feelings.** Negative feelings that we dramatize and act out include anger, sadness, and agitation. When we put on a show of our feelings, we may have an underlying agenda. Our anger shows as a tirade; our sadness huddles us into a self-pitying blob; our agitation works itself into a frenzy. What are

we really trying to communicate? There may be some hurt that is never directly addressed, covered over by a histrionic performance. We may be so excited that we revel in fantasy, only to lapse into self-pity and depression.

3. **Harbor feelings.** Sometimes we hold negative feelings inside, forming grudges and accounts against people who we feel have mistreated us. Our discontent subverts itself into negative thoughts and gossip. We let our unexpressed feelings direct our lives, as we are held hostage by those stored feelings that create ill will toward another. The person who is the object of our harbored feelings then starts to direct part of our life, draining our energy, good will, and openness for new experiences. We stagnate, until we forgive.

4. **Experience feelings.** When we are open to our experiences, they naturally flow through us, providing the energy and messages we need to lead a full life. Experiencing emotions involves trusting ourselves, knowing that the feelings are a part of us that needs expression, just as our body needs to express itself through movement. The feelings are an organic part of who we are. The more we run from those parts of us, the more we become uncomfortable with our feelings. Then we are more apt to behave erratically, mismanaging the accumulation of strong emotions. When we experience what we feel, we can regulate ourselves, releasing pent-up energy while genuinely expressing ourselves.

Feelings are often blamed for irrational thoughts and behavior. Remember, though, it is not the expression of feelings that is the problem; it is harmful behavior that causes trouble. It is the poor choices coming from certain negative feelings that create problems. For example, children can feel jealous of another's possessions. They can then explore other feelings, such as care and concern, which will override their desire to take another's things. Discussing children's thoughts with others can often help sort out their feelings. Such discussions reinforce children's positive beliefs about fairness and friendliness. Remember the sage advice that you need to feel to heal.

Children first need to become aware of their own feelings so they can understand and manage them. This self-awareness will bring confidence and self-esteem. It will help them connect with their experiences and be sensitive to how others feel.

Feelings can also be reflected in our names. Comedian George Carlin notes in his book *Brain Droppings* that names often indicate positive uplifting qualities such as Hope, Charity, and Prudence. He muses that some people should be named Grief, Hatred, and Rage.

Whatever we are feeling, it comes down to teaching ourselves to be in the moment and being aware of our experiences as we live them. By experiencing our emotions, we aren't burdened with the results of denying, dramatizing or harboring the feelings we actually have. The heart, with its vast range of emotion, is continually sending out essential feedback and lessons to help us live our lives.

THE HEART CENTER

Dr. Paul Pearsall, a psychoneuroimmunologist, has written about the wisdom and power of the heart in *The Heart's Code*. Just as science has discovered more about how the brain operates, researchers have made advances in understanding the heart. Scientists are beginning to discover what many, including indigenous cultures and Eastern medicine, have known all along. The heart is more than merely an amazing mechanical pump. The heart not only feels, but also thinks, communicates, and remembers. Just like the brain, it has cellular memories that help us love ourselves and others. The heart can connect, nurture, and integrate these memories in our cells. Where we have yet to make peace with ourselves, the heart, like the brain, experiences blockages.

Dr. Pearsall studied many heart-transplant patients and their families. He found that the subjects' lives changed after their life-saving operations. The heart-transplant recipients experienced fundamental changes, such as in their tastes in food and music, their temperaments, and their sexual interests. These changes reflected the lives of the original heart owners. Heart-transplant recipients considered their operations to have a spiritual effect, a rebirth of their life with the infusion of another person's life energy transplanted into their hearts.

In our brain-centered Western world, we have focused on analysis, technology, competition, and a separatist approach—a world of "us versus them."

When we can silence the ongoing rush of the brain, we hear the heart.

This heart connection creates a world of interrelationships, a world that works with the brain to enrich our lives. Revealingly, the heart's electromagnetic field exceeds that of the brain by five thousand times. This is a power that even the brain cannot deny.

The founding father of psychoanalysis, Sigmund Freud, recognized that "in the small matters trust the mind, in the large ones [trust] the heart." Nearly a hundred years later, we are now coming to realize how much the heart participates in our lives, how much value lies in its messages. Emotions will no longer be dismissed or equated with weakness. Feelings will be viewed as a partner to the brain, joining the thinking area that is traditionally valued in child-raising and education. The heart and its messages will no longer be a second-class citizen. It will be given its rightful place, as a key to love, health, and spiritual fulfillment. As we become more heart-centered, we will create a world in which we can better deal with our fears, cope with our hurt, and learn how to love more—a world in which we can all feel better about ourselves.

BOYS' FEELINGS, GIRLS' FEELINGS

Research is also verifying what we (especially females) have long known: Boys are less connected to their feelings than girls are. The findings are generalizations, and there are many exceptions to this overall pattern. In his books *The Wonder of Boys* and *A Fine Young Man,* Michael Gurian has admirably documented how boys have more difficulty recognizing and processing emotions. As a general rule, a girl's corpus callosum—the nerve bundle connecting the left and right brain hemispheres—is larger. Girls' stronger connection to both sides of the brain shows up on their higher scores on reading tests; on average, their verbal skills also surpass boys. Girls also do better on communication and social-skills tests.

In contrast, boys are less able to access both halves of the brain, causing them to concentrate on using the parts of the brain that specialize in logic, problem-solving, and spatial activities. Lack of full brain use can restrict boys' verbal and emotional expressions. Boys arrange their environment to create a pecking order and dominance patterns, since males prefer goal-oriented and hierarchical structures, where rules, roles, and positions are clear-cut. While helping them function, forms and protocol sometimes limit boys' awareness and potential.

Although there are many exceptions, boys are not as naturally gifted in processing emotions; they can see feelings as threatening and confusing to their identity. Male brains have traditionally functioned in hunting and gathering societies, whereas females have occupied the caregiver roles with raising children. Our society has certainly changed, but some of this orientation is hard-wired into the sexes. Of course, boys today may do their hunting in terms of chasing balls in sports activities or conquering villains in video games. Yet I have found that boys can excel at expressing feelings when they view such understanding as a task, a challenge for them to meet.

It is important for both males and females to process emotions to experience growth in life.

In addition to brain distinctions, female and male hormones account for different approaches to feelings. The estrogen/progesterone hormones cause females to cycle up and down with their moods; the male testosterone hormone drives boys more aggressively, focusing on efficient and quick solutions.

It can be argued that boys need more time to process feelings and can rebel against too much discussion of feelings. Yet as we become a more enlightened society, we will teach that recognition and expression of feelings hold a key to success in school, relationships, and career. In the meantime, the following story illustrates some further viewpoints on dealing with feelings.

DISCUSSING FEELINGS IS "RIDICULOUS NONSENSE"

Once I had a radio interview where I talked to the host about how exploring kids' feelings can be very helpful in problem-solving.

After I finished a role-play with the host on getting a child to bed, a caller phoned in to voice his opinion.

The caller angrily explained that having kids talk about feelings was "ridiculous nonsense" and a waste of time; children should basically do what they're told. He went on to say that when children grow up, they might have jobs that they don't like and can't do anything about it. He gave the example of a ditch digger, who was forced to do his job without a choice, whether he liked it or not.

The host tried to ease the man's anger, which fortunately gave me time to take stock of my own startled feelings and consider a response. I mustered my listening skills and said, "It sounds like you're angry and agitated by what I said. You do have a point about kids maybe needing more activities to wear them out before bedtime... Even if you raise a child who becomes a ditch digger, it would still be helpful for him to be aware of his feelings. He would relate better to other workers and be more in touch with his job satisfaction."

This phone caller reminded me of the traditional male role, the doer who does not have the time or interest to be aware of feelings. Our world is now making that model increasingly ineffective and obsolete.

After the interview, I privately spoke with the host, who mentioned that the caller was a regular on his show. I offered some empathy for the host. Then he said to me, "At least he acknowledged that you had a point; I've never heard him do that before." I thought that in spite of my disagreement with the caller, he still felt validated, leaving the door open for possible consideration of his own and his children's feelings.

★ TOOL 7 ★
Beginning the Feeling Exploration

Here are three ways to discuss feelings with children when they resist communicating about them:

1. **Multiple Choice:** If children are young, lack of vocabulary may account for the void; however, teenagers also often have limited vocabularies when it comes to identifying feelings. You can suggest to the youngster a multiple-choice approach, offering a variety of possible feelings to fit the situation. For example, "Are you feeling sad, hurt, angry, or confused? Which ones are you experiencing?"

2. **Wait:** A second approach to discussing feelings with children, and particularly teenagers, is to simply wait until the timing is more favorable. This may take minutes or weeks. Be alert for the right time. You may want to set up an appointed time to discuss the feelings and the surrounding situation.

3. **End Run:** A third way to open up resistant children is to focus initially on their positive emotions, instead of the times when they grapple with troublesome feelings. When kids feel positive, they are more open to communicating. Build on this positive energy. Ask them about their feelings when they laugh, rather than when they cry (or hold back the tears). Use feeling words such as: happy, joyful, content, excited, inspired, and satisfied. You are then developing vocabulary on two lev-

els: emotional understanding and word comprehension. As children grow in awareness, they are better prepared to deal with their negative feelings.

The old question "How are you feeling?" takes on a new meaning when we show genuine concern for kids. It can lead to a response that is profound and insightful. The answers then stimulate thought and feeling, resulting in communication with children. To balance communication, remember to recognize and appropriately express your own feelings on a regular basis.

A woman who attended one of my talks shared how expressing her feelings helped her earlier that day.

As the lady was preparing to come to the evening seminar, her husband arrived home and asked how she was feeling. Instead of answering automatically with the word "fine," she said, "I feel rushed." That little opening allowed her to release a lot of tension and speak her mind. She let go of stress and reconnected with herself.

Ask yourself how you are feeling right now.

DEVELOPING EMOTIONAL LITERACY

The emphasis on emotional intelligence development has begun to transform our society. Let's examine this movement on two fronts: schools and homes.

Schools. Some schools have begun introducing emotional-awareness strategies into their curricula. The results will probably improve academic performance, since children will be more aware of their feelings and how to manage them, helping them to avoid impulsive behavior. The emotional-intelligence movement—with its increased awareness of what is going on inside the person—would have impressed Socrates, who said, "The unexamined life is not worth living."

Critics of emotional literacy argue that teachers are not qualified to deal with emotions. They add that feeling good is not the aim of school. To put those criticisms in a larger context, it is time to broaden our awareness.

Teachers (as well as parents) can be trained in emotional awareness, which will help both them and children respond to learning and situations that arise in the moment. This book offers tools for such emotional literacy.

As opposed to a simplistic "feel good" approach, the educational goal can include experiencing more of the wide-ranging emotions that occur in the classroom. This emotional awareness leads to success inside and outside the classroom for both the teacher and the students.

How much more effective would teachers (and parents) be if we were more aware of our multitude of feelings, those energies that continually change and influence us as we deal with children and their feelings? In turn, how much better adjusted would children be if they could learn more about the workings of their own hearts?

Homes. Drawing from two, ten-year studies, psychology professor John Gottman taught parents how to Emotion Coach with impressive results. In *The Heart of Parenting*, he describes Emotion Coaching as cultivating an awareness of children's feelings. Gottman found that the parents who succeeded in Emotion Coaching viewed emotional expression as an opportunity for learning and intimacy. They listened with empathy and helped children find words to fit their feelings. The study also noted that successful parents used limit-setting when resolving situations with their kids. This emphasis on emotional awareness coupled with limit-setting resulted in kids improving social skills, academic performance, and even physical health.

Professor Gottman's research also identified three ways parents respond to kids' feelings that had poor results:

1. **Trivializing.** Parents were ineffective who tended to dismiss or minimize the child's difficult emotions.

2. **Disapproval.** A second unproductive approach involved caregivers who often blamed or scolded a child for negative feelings.

3. **Lack of structure.** A third ineffective style included parents who did allow children to express emotions but failed to offer guidance and limit-setting on their behavior.

We all know that difficult situations create volatile feelings in us, young and old alike. As adults, we might react abruptly with children when an uncomfortable situation confronts us. During such times, we then send the message that the way to deal with difficult circumstances is to react impulsively. When we deal with our own emotions, proactively examining them when they are more manageable, we are better able to express ourselves.

The aim is to regularly tune in to our emotions, not tune them out. As we become more comfortable with our feelings, the stronger waves of emotion can be released more appropriately in the moment. If we do respond in a hurtful way, we can take responsibility by offering apologies to the kids who have been on the receiving end of our words. From our examples, children learn how to make amends for their own actions.

We want to teach ourselves, and our children, that we can go through our feelings rather than go around them, pretending they don't exist. Again, instead of denying, harboring, or dramatizing feelings, we can experience them.

For instance, if you are uncomfortable with your thirteen-year-old attending a rock concert without adult supervision, you can share your feelings with him. You might feel worry and concern about his safety. You are then helping on two fronts: by sharing your own feelings, you are getting real with him; by caring for his safety, you are also limit-setting. To help the adolescent understand, you can disclose a time when *you* couldn't go somewhere you wanted to because of safety reasons, such as traveling to an unsafe area at night.

It is enlivening to become more emotionally literate. As emotional intelligence develops, children and adults will have greater opportunities to know themselves and those around them. Such awareness is like beaming a bright light through our present world that will carry far into the future.

FEELINGS IN THE WORKPLACE

In the competitive job market that lies ahead for children, employers cite the ability to get along with others as crucial to job success. A worker, regardless of skill level, must be emotionally compatible with others to be effective. Awareness of feelings leads to emotional well-being in the work force as well as at home and school.

If emotional maturity is so important, then why are there growing numbers of hostile-work-environment lawsuits in the

United States? These cases indicate a gap between common courtesies and cooperation and how people actually behave.

Researchers have found many workplaces to be high in incivility, which includes various disrespectful behaviors. All too commonly, workers display yelling, rudeness, and passive-aggressive behavior such as the silent treatment, not returning calls, and delaying others from getting their needs met. Bullying behavior found in the workplace can be quite personal. It includes spreading rumors and snubbing a person when a group of the other workers head off to lunch.

Managers have been found to be particularly susceptible to engaging in browbeating behavior. The key reason managers turn over (82 percent) is their inability to build good relationships with peers and subordinates. Are we teaching children how to become workers and managers, without teaching them how to work on and manage their own emotions?

The time is coming when children will not only be trained in academic subjects, but they will learn the interpersonal skills that make them successful on the job.

Employers are dealing with the same situation that parents and teachers face: You cannot mandate friendship. An unfriendly workplace reduces productivity by less work effort, lost time on the job, and turnover from changes of jobs. Perhaps more importantly, such workplaces reduce the quality of people's lives. Teaching "people skills," including emotional awareness, is becoming more a necessity rather than an extra. Revealingly, 89 percent of the workers interviewed in one study cited incivility as a serious problem in the workplace. Yet 99 percent of those workers answered that they themselves are always civil. This gap between how workers see themselves and how they see others is another indication that further training is needed.

MASKING NEGATIVE EMOTIONS

Sometimes children express that they are feeling positive at someone else's expense. For example, if a youngster takes another's food, he may say he felt "good" about seizing the food away from another. This can be perplexing (to use a feeling word) for the adult. You might wonder why he's feeling positive, when you know he should not. But he is expressing feelings, right?

Very young children may not be sensitive to what is "theirs" and what is someone else's. Their awareness of boundaries and the outside world can be too limited to have such discrimination. Older children may not have successfully completed previous developmental stages, and thus may fail to respect others' belongings.

For older children and teenagers, there are also layers of feelings underneath the "positive" feelings of taking something that belongs to another young person. Asking questions of the child will help you find more of his underlying feelings, as further outlined in Chapter 10. If the child stole the food because he wanted it, there may be some hunger needs, and poor impulse control. If he answers, "I took it because I wanted it," perhaps there were some power issues involved.

When children aggressively try to be powerful, you know they are feeling powerless. But you certainly can't accuse them of that or they will feel threatened and defensive. Instead, you can ask kids if they felt they couldn't get something they wanted.

Such questioning helps children acknowledge their feelings of powerlessness and jealousy for what someone else has. Through sensitively questioning them, you may be able to elicit their true, insecure feelings, since they will feel comfortable enough to let go of posturing and overpowering another. Remember that children may need time and space to reflect on your questions before acknowledging their weaknesses.

There are times when you need to use yourself as a model. Set your values—such as honesty and limit-setting—for children to understand what is healthy. By defining standards you help them along a path they will enjoy, even if they don't immediately understand the structure you are providing.

Here is an example of how to help children learn boundaries and positive feelings. The exchange occurred between a fifteen-year-old boy and myself in one of my classes.

> During a class project, the students were all blowing bubbles, an experience that preceded a creative-writing lesson. Instead of observing the phenomenon, Jack went around blowing bubbles in his peers' faces, which made him laugh as others winced. I called Jack aside and talked with him.
>
> "Jack, how did you feel when you were blowing bubbles in your peers' faces?"
>
> "I felt good; it was funny."
>
> "How did your peers feel?"
>
> "They didn't mind; it was only a joke."
>
> "Did you know that you were getting in your peers' boundaries—their private space—by blowing your bubbles in their faces?"
>
> "Well, yes."
>
> "Are you respecting their space?"
>
> "I don't know."
>
> "I'm wondering: Are you ever disrespected?"

Jack's cool veneer suddenly turned hot. He raised his voice, saying, "Yes, plenty of times! Like when people take my things."

"You don't like that." Jack nodded and I continued. "When you invade your peers' space, it's really not so funny."

"Yeah, I guess so."

"When you disrespect your peers' space, how do they feel?"

"Uncomfortable."

"And how do *you* really feel?"

"Uncomfortable." Jack nodded and looked toward the floor.

"What could you do next time?"

"Respect their space," he said, looking up.

"Would that make you feel more secure and respected?"

"Yes."

EXPRESSING FEELINGS

Listen to kids' feelings, the ones on the surface and those underneath. Helping them reflect over their behavior can gently bring out their insecurities, the awkwardness that they might mask through sarcasm, bullying, and aggression. Stay away from judging and attacking their character and self-worth. Help kids develop character by putting their behavior in the context of positive values, such as trust, respect, and responsibility. By listening and guiding, you can help them see themselves more clearly. This supportive structure will lead them to better choices and decisions—and genuine positive feelings.

The goal is not just to express feelings, but also to know when and how to express feelings. As we all become more aware of our own feelings, we become more aware of how others feel. This self-awareness provides us with an intuitive sense of timing about emotions. The more children—and adults—can appropriately express various feelings, the more problems get solved, the more confidence grows, and the better equipped we all are to deal with living our lives and creating a brighter future.

Let's examine, then, one of the most potent and volatile feelings children and adults experience: anger. How much better would everyone's life be if this complex emotion was understood and well managed?

CHAPTER EIGHT

Handling Anger

Anger is a powerful emotion. This rush of energy can be used destructively or constructively. It can be a mask, hiding underlying feelings and distorted thoughts. Or, it can be a flag, signaling that our needs are not being met.

Let's probe how anger can be used as a mask to conceal thoughts and feelings, or a flag to alert us. This chapter offers a variety of ways to understand anger, for yourself and for your children. It also provides specific tools to channel this emotion into a healthy, constructive expression and heal what hurts underneath.

Anger, like other feelings, connects us to our needs and desires when we learn how to use it, as Tool 14 explores. Misused, however, it becomes a defense mechanism. Anger then keeps others at a distance, as it conceals feelings and uses faulty thinking.

ANGER AND SOCIETY

Let's look at different ways that anger manifests itself in American society.

1. **Media.** Angry people in news stories and entertainment shows rarely talk out their problems. In knee-jerk fashion, television and movies usually show violent responses to conflict, suggesting violence as the only solution. Studies reveal that three out of every five TV programs contain violence; and 89 percent of TV movies depict violent solutions to interpersonal conflicts. Cartoons overflow with violent situations as well. That is why many have advised caregivers to supervise and limit kids' access and time in viewing media.

2. **School.** In the 1997-1998 school year, it was found that nearly a million U.S. students in grades 6-12 carried a gun to school. Nearly half of those students were armed in school six or more times.

   Research has shown what constitutes effective anti-violence programs for schools. Strategies that work emphasize positive norms, which means teaching about healthy normal behavior. Students learn that although many children have carried guns to school, this is still a small fraction compared to the total number of students. Aggression and violence are shown as neither normal nor acceptable behavior. To avert violence, schools can teach life skills such as handling teasing and bullying and learning anger management. Studies also find that involving everyone, including parents, peers, media and community organizations, further prevents violence. To create safer schools, one study recommended teaching basic emotional skills by age four.

3. **Computer and Video Games.** In addition to media and school violence, many kids take a more interactive role in violence through some video and computer games. Playing these games can easily become addictive, like watching television. James Alan Fox, dean of the College of Criminal Justice at Northeastern University, says, "Rather than watch people get shot, kids can do the shooting. In the mind of many kids, the line between virtual reality and reality is pretty thin... I think [violent computer games] reflect the...tip of youth violence caused by inadequate adult supervision, excessive access to dangerous weapons, and a steady diet of violent entertainment."

It reminds me of the cartoon with two teenagers looking at a dead Uncle Sam that one of them had just shot. The corpse was carrying a sign that read "Stop Violence." Now the protest sign lay atop Uncle Sam's lifeless body. The teenager who was holding the smoking gun says to his friend, "He was bugging me."

4. **Adults as Models.** In addition to how media and video games affect anger, we need to look at our own anger management and how that influences young people. Children's temper can be a mirror to understand how we express anger and what gets us upset. Children's difficulties—their insecurity, their poor self-esteem—may be reflecting part of us. For instance, if we are yelling, we can hardly expect children to act calmly. We may also be at risk of hurting kids due to our own volatile impulses. Like water reaching a boil, we need to back off and let things cool down. Remember that we all have unresolved issues, so finding time to deal with our own anger should be a priority. As we come to know ourselves better, we are better able to help ourselves and our children learn and grow.

HELPING KIDS WITH ANGER

The psychologist Haim Ginott offered these helpful principles: All feelings are permissible, but not all behaviors are permissible. And it is up to the adult to define permissible behavior so the child understands safe limits. A young person can have negative and destructive thoughts or wishes, but the line must be drawn: He needs to refrain from acting on such desires. When anger is controlled, it serves as a powerful means for self-expression. When it is uncontained and coupled with reckless behavior, the results are regrettable.

As you explore a young person's difficulty, it is helpful to find the source if possible. Yet such explorations can require allowing enough time and patience to achieve results.

Anger is far more manageable at its inception than after it gets repressed and ignored.

In the grips of anger, a person's reasoning ability can be temporarily blocked. You can observe such features as loud voice, flushed cheeks, clenched fists, flared nostrils, widened eyes, and rapid breathing. These are clues that the child is not composed enough to talk with you in an acceptable way.

There is an idea about releasing anger by "ventilation": The more you "vent" and express anger, the more it is released. However, research has shown such behavior to be a poor way of resolving anger. Clearly, it is helpful to release energy through physical means such as walking or running. Exercise helps a person calm down. Yet when anger has underlying issues, the disturbed feelings will predictably return until sufficiently handled. Just "venting" anger in the form of loud or destructive behavior can actually increase aggression. A person then can fly more into a rage, with possible abusive results, as the anger issues forth unchecked.

If the youth is swearing and insulting you, you don't have to stand there and take it. A time out may be in order. When you do talk with the young person, offer acceptable ways for him to express his anger. If he still is not willing to calm down, you can say, "I won't accept your rude behavior. I'll come back when you're calmer." Just be sure the youngster continues to have appropriate supervision. If you cannot leave altogether, physically distance yourself from the young person. It can take time for a child—or an adult—to calm down.

When the discussion does occur, your listening skills will be invaluable. Your timing and patience will create a positive atmosphere. Answers will then naturally emerge from your exploration, rather than pushing for some conclusion or exhausting analysis.

Studies have shown that being able to recognize unsettling feelings helps children's resiliency, giving them more resources to deal with stressful situations.

By encouraging children to
express anger in an appropriate way,
you help them grow emotionally
and intellectually.

The more we create an atmosphere of exploring feelings, good listening skills, and solid, reasonable boundaries, the more we can help young people deal with their anger appropriately. Help children realize their emotions, including anger, are natural, and that feelings can be appropriately expressed without resulting in negative behavior.

TWO PROACTIVE APPROACHES TO ANGER

To handle anger, with its power and volatility, you can be proactive instead of reactive. Here are two ways to defuse and redirect anger:

1. **Detach yourself.** If the anger is directed at you, pretend that the child is upset at someone else. This can help you be more objective. It is easier to deal with the situation if you imagine the child is angry at another person instead of yourself.

2. **Find specifics.** Ask the youngster to be specific about what makes him angry. He might say "everything" in that angry moment. Then ask him to give one example, one specific. Finding particular points helps break down the wall of anger, allowing unrecognized feelings and needs to surface.

Here is a story that illustrates how these two techniques can be applied.

During a basketball practice, one of my students revealed his disturbed feelings about me. Thirteen-year-old Max was angry with some of my basketball coaching and made a series of loud, rude remarks on the court. I asked him to cool down in a time out area away from the others. When I joined him, Max told me about his hatred of me. "I don't know. I hate the way you do things. I hate everything about you. You don't teach like other teachers."

I took a deep breath and exhaled, letting my student's words settle. I deliberately thought of his anger as if it were directed at someone else. I also steadied myself by consciously breathing and remembering that my feet were on the ground.

"What's one thing you don't like about what I do?"

"Everything!"

"Name one thing you don't like."

"Well, you made us do that stupid basketball drill."

I avoided going into the convincing mode, which would just be an attempt to justify myself. Trying to make my point would evoke opposition in him and defensiveness in me. Instead, I wanted him to know that I had listened to him. Using a neutral tone, I decided to offer a summary of what he had said.

"So I'm different from other teachers, and that bothers you. Sometimes I ask you to do things that you haven't done before."

Max nodded, indicating that his thoughts had been validated and his feelings had been acknowledged. I noticed that after I responded to his remarks, his body relaxed in the chair and his facial muscles eased. His body language, the nonverbal behavior, showed signs of releasing tension.

I checked my own feelings at this point, and realized I felt relieved and confident that Max was ready to act sociably and participate in class. Rather than telling him, I asked him the following: "I'm wondering if we can work together, since we will be spending time in the classroom together. Can we try that?"

Max nodded and returned to the class. His anger had dissolved and he was ready to participate. By talking about what specifically disturbed him, his wall of anger had broken down. Max realized he had let the way I set up the basketball plays threaten his well-being. His anger had been expressed, heard, and validated. By allowing unrecognized feelings to surface, he calmed down and became cooperative. Appropriately channeled anger builds character. It's also nice to know that Max no longer hates everything about me.

Focus on the specific issue(s) behind the anger, the ones that fuel its intensity. Explore what supports the anger's intensity. In Max's case, our discussion helped him connect more with his feelings. He also handled his thoughts of inadequacy, even if only on an intuitive level. When children express their inner experience without being criticized or shamed by another, they feel accepted. Kids are then empowered to know themselves and release tension. Allow this free expression within the limits of safety and respect.

Drawing good boundaries with children helps them define acceptable behavior. They then can develop their own self-control, building a sense of security, knowing you won't allow them to lapse into poor self-control. You are teaching them how to interact with others, getting in touch with their own feelings while respecting others. Bridges are built as children improve their ability to communicate, helping themselves and others.

A LESSON ON THE TENNIS COURT

Unchecked anger can degenerate into abusive words and destructive behavior. Although anger releases a powerful adrenaline rush, it can hurt the person unleashing the anger as well as the person on the receiving end. When anger is used as a weapon, it can set off a destructive cycle. It then leads to more conflict instead of finding a solution.

The hurt caused by explosive anger can last far past the incident, sometimes for many years. In the case of kids, if they are allowed to express abusive remarks without check, where will this lead them? How will they treat others, including their children and those with whom they are in intimate relationships?

We also will benefit from examining ourselves to find areas where our own anger gets out of control. When we are controlled by our fury, then we may say hurtful things to others. The key is to express anger appropriately, not suppress it or let it become an instrument of destruction.

The sound and the fury of anger reminds me of when I took a group of my students—all emotionally disturbed adolescent boys—to play tennis one warm summer day.

As we approached the two courts, I noticed an elderly man standing with his dog on the sideline. The man and the small brown dog were along the fence in the shade. Since the man had no tennis gear, I was going to ask him if he was using the one court. I walked over to him with my students trailing behind me; they were probably wondering how their teacher would handle this real-life situation outside the classroom.

Standing ten feet away from him, I noticed his pencil-thin mustache widen as his mouth tightened. Before I could speak, sounds exploded from his mouth: He had begun to unleash a string of curses at me. The tirade focused on how he thought I was going to take the court away from him. It took me a moment to recover from his stream of invectives to realize how angry, and afraid, this man was of losing his space on the court. Perhaps I was able to keep my own composure because I was in a state of partial shock. At some point during his outburst, I gathered that he wanted to train his dog in the shady area of the tennis court.

Fortunately, one of my students, Alan, chimed in. Alan suggested that we could take one court, leaving the man with his dog on the other court. I repeated this timely solution to the man. He stopped his tirade, which was a relief, to consider the suggestion. Suddenly he began swearing again, saying that we were going to take the court that had shade.

I firmly responded, "Sir, I don't appreciate your abusive comments. Please control your language... Okay, then, we can take the sunny court."

The man muttered something, but I knew he had heard that I wouldn't tolerate his aggressive anger toward me. He went over to the shaded tennis court to walk his dog. Afterward, we took our designated court and the tennis proceeded with no further problems. Ten minutes later, the old man left, with his little dog trailing behind him.

It was an interesting lesson that day. My special-education students were shocked that another adult would act so rudely to their teacher. They probably understood on some level that they, like the old man, acted unfriendly toward others at times. Yet no one wanted to end up like that poor old guy, barking obscenities at a teacher with his impressionable students on a public tennis court. It's a lesson I took to heart as well.

★ TOOL 8 ★
Defusing Anger

To help decipher our experiences, here is a powerful technique for understanding and releasing anger. When using it with a child, you might need to help the young person through it. This tool is based on finding out the needs and feelings, often unconscious, that connect with the anger. Using this approach leads to a powerful sense of empathy for oneself and for others, which creates solutions on how to resolve the situation.

Anger signals that our needs are not getting met. We often confuse or mask our real needs by blaming others or considering ourselves helpless victims. When we can discover our real needs and what we can do about them, we become happy and content, at least until another need is put in jeopardy.

Sometimes, instead of a need being at stake, there is a desire that triggers the anger. Do you know anyone who has become angry when not getting ice cream or being unable to watch a TV show? These are examples of unfulfilled desires. Admittedly, we have difficulty when we don't get what we want, but children have even more difficulty when their desires remain unfulfilled. In such cases, you can establish for kids the difference between what is a need (see Needs Inventory) and what is a desire. Here is a guideline: If it's not a need, it's probably a desire.

To create balance, help children fulfill their needs and moderate their desires.

This anger-resolution tool expresses a needs/ feelings/ action sequence. The exercise uses a statement describing the anger, followed by answering a series of related questions. The concluding part, the action plan, usually emerges naturally from the preceding parts. The action plan often includes the person's finding a way to acceptably compromise. After gaining insights about the needs and feelings involved, the participant now accepts the situation that once sparked anger and discontent.

A note: This process works well with adults' anger as well as children's anger.

First, complete the following sentence. "I get angry when..." Express your anger as a description of what situation or behavior triggers your anger. Avoid name-calling or belittling another. An appropriate anger statement for an adult and a child respectively might be, "I get angry when you don't clean your dishes"; "I get angry when I have to clean my room."

Second, ask the following three questions about your original anger statement:

1. **NEEDS/DESIRES:**

   - Ask this question of yourself: What needs or desires am I trying to satisfy?

   - If the anger connects with another's behavior, ask: What needs or desires is that person trying to satisfy when he acts in a way that evokes my anger? (See Table 8.1.)

   - Note the relationship between the other person's needs and desires and your own.

TABLE 8.1
NEEDS INVENTORY

- Safety and security: air, light, food, water, shelter, clothing

- Movement and exercise

- Recreation

- Belonging

- Nurturing

- Self-esteem and respect

- Communication of thoughts and feelings

- Creativity

- Spiritual fulfillment

---

2. **FEELINGS:**

- How do you feel on the inside? (See Table 8.2.)

- To gather empathy for the person who provokes your anger, ask: How does that person feel on the inside when behaving in a way that makes you angry?

3. **ACTION PLAN:**

- What can you do to handle your anger?

This approach will help you see how your needs can mirror the other person's needs. For example, if the other person needs security, you might have the same need at stake. By developing empathy, this technique can provide the understanding of self and others that transforms anger. It helps you separate from your own anger, seeing it from a more objective perspective. You may not approve of your own or the other person's behavior, but you now have a way to understand your experience. This approach can let your anger lead to acceptance and appropriate action.

Here is an example of how this powerful technique plays out. The key statements and questions are in italics.

A teenager, fifteen-year-old Joe, told me, "*I get angry when* adults order me around because I'm a young man and don't need to be ordered around like a little kid." Joe spoke in a harsh, loud voice.

What do you need? [your needs] "I need to be respected."

How come the adults order you around? What do you think their needs are? [their needs] "They probably are trying to help me out when they tell me what to do."

How are you feeling when they order you around? [your feelings] "I feel hurt and disturbed."

TABLE 8.2
FEELINGS INVENTORY

AFRAID	ANGRY	HURT	POWERLESS
Awed	Annoyed	Aching	Depressed
Appalled	Bitter	Afflicted	Disbelieving
Awkward	Boiling	Agonized	Empty
Cowardly	Cross	Crushed	Exhausted
Dismayed	Enflamed	Despairing	Failing
Doubtful	Enraged	Distressed	Frustrated
Fearful	Fuming	Hapless	Guilty
Frightened	Incensed	Heartbroken	Helpless
Isolated	Indignant	Injured	Hopeless
Lonely	Infuriated	Mournful	Isolated
Menaced	Irritated	Offended	Lethargic
Out of place	Offended	Pained	Longing
Panicked	Provoked	Piteous	Numb
Quaking	Resentful	Sad	Regretful
Timid	Stewing	Suffering	Restless
Restless	Sulky	Tortured	Shamed
Shaky	Worked up	Victimized	Shocked
Threatened	Wrathful	Vulnerable	Sorrowful
		Worried	Tearful

How does the person feel on the inside when he is "ordering you around?" [their feelings] "When they are acting all tough around me, they probably feel hurt and weak on the inside." [If the child has trouble answering, you can offer suggestions.]

What can you do to handle your anger when adults tell you what to do? [action plan] "I can try to understand and cope with it." Joe's voice had now softened as his body posture relaxed.

After describing his anger, Joe was able to empathize with the adults who had disturbed him. He also gathered the inner resolve to deal with his situation in a calm manner. His sense of powerlessness was mirrored in the behavior of the adult who had "ordered" him around.

Joe summoned the inner will to accept others and accept himself. Some children will need help identifying others' needs as well as their own. Their anger and identification may be inappropriately expressed by blaming and name-calling those who anger them. This anger-management exercise provides tools to identify their real needs and then find a way to meet them in a healthy way.

Troubleshooting the Process

What if there does not seem to be any compromise for an action plan?

To illustrate, here is how one set of parents dealt with their nine-year-old daughter's anger about being unable to have a pet dog. The parents denied their daughter the pet because there was no available space in the house. The daughter's needs were belonging and security; her parents' needs were security and freedom of movement. Both parents and child felt hurt—the parents for not providing a dog and the child for being denied a pet.

TABLE 8.3
JOE'S ANGER PROCESS

Anger Statement:

"I get angry when adults order me around because I'm a young man and don't need to be ordered around like a little kid."

Needs/Desires Identification:

- *Joe's needs*: Security, self-esteem and respect.

- *Adults' needs (those which connect with his anger)*: Security and self-esteem.

Feelings Identification:

- *Joe's feelings:* Insecure and hurt.
- *Adults' feelings:* Insecure and hurt.

Action Plan:

Joe can be more understanding of those who give him directions, and better control his own temper. He can also ask for more explanation about what he's expected to do. Perhaps he can suggest that the adult explain it differently, in a less demanding way. The details of such a plan may need to be worked out with an adult.

Even though getting a dog was not negotiable, an action plan emerged: getting a pet turtle. This pet took little space and lived in the back yard.

What if there is absolutely no possibility for alternatives or compromise? To again illustrate, a ten-year-old boy was angry that he had to clean his bathroom. He had needs of respect and self-expression, while his caregiver also had need of respect, as well as the security of a well-kept house. The youngster felt angry, stubborn, and disappointed; the caregiver felt determined and rushed. The boy realized the action plan was simply to express his thoughts and feelings (an often overlooked need), even if he still had to clean the bathroom. Realizing that he could express himself relieved the pressure and created understanding and acceptance. Sometimes just talking about feelings and thoughts is the action plan, even if the rest of the situation remains unchanged.

By doing this anger-resolution process, my adolescent students have expressed some insightful comments that included:

- I learned that there are other options besides yelling.

- Both people [involved in the situation] have their own separate needs.

- Everyone's feelings count.

- I can handle things appropriately.

Finding constructive ways to express anger allows people to feel clearer and balanced, more in charge of their lives without being at the mercy of others and their own reactionary impulses. This anger-management technique makes sense of the senselessness of anger; it offers structure to anger's chaos. It also finds reasonable ways to work with your own needs as well as ways of getting along with others. As unconscious needs, desires, and feelings are worked out, children and adults can move past anger, experiencing learning and growth.

Now you can experience this approach to dealing with anger. Try it out on yourself and with a child. Go through the anger statement and three follow-up questions, concerning the needs and feelings of all people involved and the resulting action plan. Write them down. Reflect on the needs, feelings, and solutions that emerge. They may stimulate other profound discussions, insights, and connections. As angry feelings are allowed appropriate expression, more peace and understanding will replace conflict and violence in our lives.

TAKING RESPONSIBILITY FOR OUR ANGER

In 1972 Dr. Haim Ginott wrote in *Teacher & Child: A Book for Parents and Teachers* that teachers are not prepared for the anger they will experience in themselves while dealing with children. Several decades after Dr. Ginott wrote that warning, his words still hold true for anyone who works or lives with kids. We are still not trained or prepared for our own anger in dealing with children.

There are signs of change, however, such as the emotional intelligence movement that has begun. As we have discussed, learning how to express feelings creates self-knowledge and confidence to succeed throughout life.

Dr. Ginott had some excellent advice in his *Teacher & Child* book. Although he addresses teachers in this passage, anyone who works or lives with kids can benefit from this advice:

> An enlightened teacher [or parent] is not afraid of his anger, because he has learned to express it without doing damage. He has mastered the secret of expressing anger without insult. Even un-

der provocation he does not call the children abusive names. He does not attack their character or offend their personality. He does not tell them whom they resemble and where they will end up. *When angry...he describes what he sees, what he feels, and what he expects* [italics mine].

Dr. Ginott recommended using "I messages" to take responsibility for your own anger. For example, "I am frustrated when you keep entering the classroom in a loud voice." Or "I am disturbed by how much you tease your sister." Saying "I" replaces the accusing word "you," which blames another person for your feelings. Examples of using "you" for blame are: "You are a spoiled brat," or "You're no good and worthless." In contrast, using "I" takes responsibility for yourself and how you feel: "I feel disrespected when you keep asking me to buy things for you"; and "I get concerned when you sit around and watch television so much."

By asserting how you feel without blaming the youngster, you are honestly dealing with your own feelings. No one can argue with you if you say you are angry. But you can easily set people on the defensive by saying you are a "so-and-so," which belittles their character.

★ TOOL 9 ★
Using "I Statements" to Express Anger

This next tool is a follow-up on "I statements," helping a person take responsibility for his or her anger without degrading another. It is a good method for adults as well as children to learn.

The exercise starts with an *inappropriate* anger statement, followed by an *appropriate* "I statement" that includes a suggestion on how to deal with the situation. Remember, "I statements" start with owning your feelings, followed by a description of the behavior that stirred the angry feelings. Anger connects to many feelings, so you can be hurt, worried, annoyed, confused, uncomfortable, and so on. The second half of the exercise allows space for you to come up with your own appropriate anger statements.

INAPPROPRIATE ANGER	APPROPRIATE ANGER
1. Your room is always a mess.	I get irritated when I see your room messy. What can you do to keep the house looking better?
2. Just this once, tell the truth.	I am disappointed when you lie to me. I want to be able to trust you to tell the truth. I know you can tell the truth.
3. How rude! You always interrupt.	It frustrates me when you interrupt my conversation. Please wait unless it's a real emergency. Remember to say, "Excuse me" when you have to say something while someone else is talking.

4. Don't you know anything?   I'm concerned that you're having trouble with your work. Who could help you?

5. You think money grows on trees!   I get disturbed when you expect me to keep buying you so many things. I work hard for our money. Is there a way you can earn money, or how can you live without what you want right now?

The following five examples are left blank for you to complete.

6. You're never home on time.   6.

7. You don't know the meaning of the word "respect."   7.

8. All you ever do is argue.   8.

9. You're impossible!   9.

10. Can't you be more responsible?   10.

Notice how the inappropriate comments in the left-hand column demean the person. They send the message that the youngster is a hopeless failure, somehow irreparably flawed. Although we may sometimes have those thoughts about others, such as our kids, it is unhealthy to put our feelings in such a negative context, which denies a person's self-worth and potential. Inappropriate anger about another can be a mirror for the negative messages we say to ourselves. The "I messages" on the right give a structure for emotions, so our feelings can connect with positive thoughts as well as constructive and necessary feedback for the other person. It is equally valuable to have kids as well as adults learn "I statements".

"I messages" promote a healthy release of anger by describing the events and behavior that are anger-producing. This approach helps us express our feelings without attacking a person's character and self-worth.

ANGER AS AN ALLY

As we claim our own anger, we can direct this tension, finding ways to connect with positive feelings and workable solutions. We no longer need to use anger as a mask to conceal ourselves; instead we can use it to flag our needs. In dealing with children, we then become free to communicate openly and directly. We can also teach kids how to claim their own anger—and to choose appropriate actions when angry.

Anger contains a powerful energy. When we effectively respond to its call, anger can be a great ally. We need to educate ourselves and children about its messages. Managing anger averts violence, resolves problems, and builds self-confidence. In the process, we then find the underlying issues signaled by anger.

In this chapter, we have considered many ways to be proactive with anger:

- Detaching ourselves when we are the object of a child's anger.

- Breaking down a child's wall of anger to find out the specific concern.

- Using anger management processes: the defusing anger technique and "I statements."

Let's commit to teaching ourselves and our kids how to use anger so it does not use us. To offer further assistance, the next chapter explores healthy boundaries.

CHAPTER NINE

Setting Good Boundaries

In teaching special education for many years—much of the time with emotionally disturbed adolescent boys—I noticed a habit that students often unknowingly displayed when they first entered my class. While talking with me at my desk, they would pick up objects from the desk, such as pencils, ornaments, or materials. This habit was unconscious; the students touched my things without thinking. They did not ask to look at my things, nor was the conversation even about the objects they handled without permission.

When a student would handle one of my belongings, I would interject, "Did you ask to touch that?" He would suddenly stop, put down the object that he handled, and say, "No." Often he would continue to touch the things after repeated reminders. This behavior told me that if a mild intervention, like a reminder, did not work, then it was time for a stronger intervention. Thus I would inform the student that the next time he touched something without permission, I would send him on a time out (in a separated area) to think about his behavior. That usually stopped his impulsive touching and helped him to respect my things.

Touching others' possessions is not limited to special-education students. Setting boundaries begins in early childhood, distinguishing what is and what is not part of the child. Healthy boundaries are integral to a person's individuation. Yet many children, way past the toddler stage, still have not learned where they end and the rest of the world begins. Their desires and impulses blur the distinction between what belongs to them and what belongs to others.

★ TOOL 10 ★
Defining Boundaries

Here are questions you can ask kids when they need further help on recognizing and establishing good boundaries. Dealing with the following series of questions will help increase their awareness of physical boundaries:

- **Consequences.** Ask about the consequences of touching others' items without permission. Children might respond that their friends don't mind if they touch their things. Then ask, "Can you touch anything of theirs, such as their money or valuables in their pockets?" This question will give children pause for thought...and reflection.

- **How would they feel.** Ask children if anybody could be upset if their things were touched without permission. Ask them about the possibility of their damaging or taking another's things by accident or on purpose. Delve into what the upset person might do when discovering his or her items were touched without permission. Possible answers may be anger, distrust, and retaliatory actions such as people going through the children's own belongings. Using a neutral tone, ask if they want these kinds of consequences.

- **What they learned.** In conclusion, ask what they have learned about boundaries and others' belongings (which can include another person's body). Listen carefully to kids' words and summarize what they say. It might be something like "I guess I should leave other people's things alone unless I ask." Those words are invaluable, since they come from children themselves, showing an internal understanding and self-responsibility in the matter.

Here is an easy explanation of boundaries for children: Tell them there is *you*—your body and possessions—and the rest of the world is *not* you. Afterward, children can be politely instructed to ask permission if they want to touch anything that does not belong to them.

To further establish good boundaries, the child should ask *before* touching. For example, if a youngster wants to look at a calculator, she should not pick it up before asking if she can use it. Rather, the child should first ask if she could use it, then *after* receiving permission, pick it up. "Thanks, Sheila, for asking if you could use that. I appreciate your having good boundaries. It shows I can trust you. Since you asked, you may look at it." [Or "Thanks for asking, but you may not look at it because (and then explain the reason)."] That builds the child's confidence. In the future, keep reinforcing the young person's positive behavior of asking permission before she touches something.

OTHER BOUNDARIES

In addition to the physical ones, emotional and intellectual boundaries need attention. Some boundaries—such as not discussing a person's income, weight or age—may vary from person to person. Children should be sensitized to these areas. Such awareness training can include discussions on why those areas can be touchy for some people, whether for personal reasons or societal customs. Also, help children become aware of times when a person is not ready to talk about upsetting changes, such as a divorce or the death of a loved one. This behavior demonstrates respect for the boundaries of the person's personal and emotional space.

Teaching healthy boundaries by example and instruction is part of our role with children. We demonstrate respect for their things as part of the exchange. Consider ways to set firm and reasonable boundaries, demonstrating them in a clear and caring manner. As young people come to know what is theirs and what is someone else's, they function better—and are better prepared for the uncharted boundaries their future will bring.

BUILDING ON YOUR FOUNDATION

In concluding this second part of the book, "Getting to the Basics," we have developed listening skills. We also explored ways to help children know their feelings, manage anger, and establish trust and boundaries. The next part of the book takes this strong foundation and offers many ways for children to build healthy relationships. The theme of our own awareness and development also continues through this next part, "Making Growth Choices."

Part 3

MAKING GROWTH CHOICES

*Every blade of grass
has an angel that bends over it
and whispers "Grow! Grow!"*

- THE TALMUD

CHAPTER TEN

Encouraging Kids to Answer

There are some revealing statistics on how children learn. Children retain only 20 percent of what they hear; yet they retain 70 percent of what they say. Notice the big jump in learning when kids get to talk about a subject rather than just hearing someone else talk about it. When children both say and do something, the retention rate rises to 90 percent.

These statistics bear out common sense and experience. For instance, would you learn more by hearing someone talk about a food dish, or would you learn far more by explaining the recipe while you made the dish?

To help communicate with kids, see if they can come up with the answer themselves. Our discussions with children benefit from drawing them out, allowing them to develop their own problem-solving skills.

DAVE'S STORY

Here is a story of how I encouraged a student to find some of his own answers.

One of my teenage students, Dave, had a habit of trying to impress his peers in health class. Whenever we would talk about social issues such as dating, he would phrase his answers in such a way that you might think he was a teenage Don Juan and MTV star.

When it came time to talk with him privately about his bragging in class, I knew that Dave could easily become defensive. To help him be more receptive, I began our discussion by using the example of another teenager, a fictional character I called Milo. I told Dave how Milo would tell his peers during class discussions how great he was at basketball. In actuality, I continued to explain, Milo was only an average player, but since no one in the class played ball with him, his basketball exploits could not be verified. Similarly, no one could verify Dave's sexual exploits, since in this case, his peers were not in social situations with him now and did not know his past.

I questioned Dave about how Milo, the bragging ball player, must have felt. After some exploring, Dave said that Milo probably felt insecure and was trying to make up for it by trying to impress others. I nodded, refraining from pointing out how Dave, too, was insecure and trying to impress his peers in class.

I redirected the conversation back to Dave by asking him, "In class, what do you think about the way you describe your relationships with girls? Do you think that could ever come across as bragging?" Dave then felt comfortable enough to admit he was trying to make up for what he considered a lack in himself. He came to the answer without my telling him—this made the answer golden.

I could have told him the answer by saying, "Dave, you're trying to impress your peers. You don't have to feel insecure like that." But how would he have responded? Such a direct approach would have made Dave defensive and argumentative. He would have retained 20 percent of what I said, but missed an opportunity to reach his own understanding and seek a solution for himself.

To conclude our discussion, I asked Dave to visualize how he would be acting in the next health class. Using his auditory sense, he heard himself speaking in more modest terms. He said he felt more relaxed and natural. The following days in class, Dave's answers were appropriate, without boasts and embellishments. His subsequent classroom behavior supported this more humble image of himself.

When children speak and visualize, expressing the answers themselves, their understanding dramatically increases.

The interactive approach in this example relates to the roots of education, which come from the Latin verb *educare*, meaning "to draw out." This was the way Socrates would approach people: He would ask others questions, so they could discover the answer for themselves. Like Socrates, we can help kids discover answers for themselves.

ASKING INSTEAD OF TELLING

Here is a wonderful way to have kids discover the answers for themselves. Instead of giving your message as a statement, convert it into a question. For example, instead of telling your daughter what time she needs to come home, *ask* her when would be a reasonable time to return, knowing the family standards as she does. Furthermore, instead of telling her of the consequences if she returns late, *ask* her what the consequences will be if she is late.

If you disagree with her answer, then a further question would be in order. If she ultimately responds that no consequence should be given, you might say, "You will receive some consequence. What consequence would be fair if you broke your agreement about arriving home on time?"

If the young person still will not give an acceptable answer, you can respond, "Well, since you haven't come up with a reasonable answer, you're asking [note that word] me to come up with a consequence. If you arrive late, you will not be able to go out this weekend [or whatever consequence is reasonable and appropriate for the situation]."

Sometimes the child will impose too harsh a consequence on herself. That is a good time to teach moderation and consequences to fit the situation. "No, staying in for a whole month is too long. I believe one week would be fairer and more appropriate." Chapter 15 explores the subject of consequences and interventions to help children.

Here are other examples of helping kids discover answers for themselves. Instead of "You know you're not supposed to touch that painting!" try asking, "Should you touch that painting, especially considering that the sign says 'No touching'? What might happen if you touched it?" Instead of reprimanding the youngster with "Don't sit on that basketball!" try asking, "What might happen if you keep sitting on that basketball?"

By telling children what to do, we can easily slip into the lecturing mode. In contrast, asking them questions invites self-examination and develops thinking and sensitivity to others.

To get your message across, use a neutral tone of voice when asking. A question asked in a sarcastic or demeaning tone is not really a sincere question; it is just telling again, with the added weight of belittling the young person.

When you ask questions of children, you are like an investigator trying to find out what makes sense in the situation. "Is it a good idea to grab the ketchup or is there a better way to do it?" Such an approach gives them space and dignity, building self-esteem as children are empowered to choose without coercion.

> *It helps children to realize that there are consequences, positive and negative, for the choices they make.*

A note: Try to phrase your questions in a way that clearly conveys your message to the child. For example, if you want to have the child remember when it's bedtime, you can ask, "What time do you go to bed?" Even though the child may not like the appointed time, the youngster is still taking responsibility by answering the question. This avoids power struggles and validates the child. Your message and limit-setting will be lost, however, if you ask, "Would you like to go to bed at nine?" This kind of open-ended question invites arguments and dissension.

★ TOOL 11 ★
Turn Telling Into Asking

Here are steps to convert telling into asking:

1. Review a recent time when you needed to inform or correct a young person. Write down what you said and how the child responded. Evaluate how effectively you communicated. Did you talk too much? How much did the child listen? Did you slip into a lecturing style?

2. Rework your talk, this time formulating your message into a series of questions. Write down your questions and compare them to what you originally said. How do they compare? Do they get your message across? Can you be more precise, or offer additional questions for clarity?

3. Practice asking your questions in an appropriate tone, free of moralizing or sarcasm.

4. Plan for the next time you need to communicate with a child about some area that needs explanation or correction. Develop a series of questions to help the child think about your point.

After delivering your series of question, record the experience. What worked? What could have been improved? How well did the child listen and understand? How can you evaluate the child's receptivity to your approach? How did this question-asking approach compare with the answer-giving approach you previously used?

Here is what a woman told me after one of my workshops:

I raised two children from my second marriage. This time I wanted to make it a good experience, and continually give them positive suggestions. But I now realize that they are teens, and I am giving them too many answers. By asking them questions, they can then get the answers themselves.

To continue this learning cycle, you can feed back to children their realizations after they have already found their own answers. *Their* answers then become the material for the positive suggestions you offer, enhancing their growth and self-esteem.

HOW TO AVOID LECTURING

One of the most common ways to silence kids is by lecturing them. A lecture can range from a moralizing talk to a tirade. Its key characteristics, when used as an inappropriate way to correct behavior, include yelling, insulting, and nonstop talking.

To understand the impact of lecturing, ask yourself the following questions: Have you ever liked it when someone gave you a lecture? When you were on the receiving end of the lecture, how did you feel? How do you think children feel when they receive lectures? In the case of lecturing to kids, our words and tone take on added weight because adults are more powerful and usually larger in size than children.

Lecturing tends to degrade others, causing kids to deal awkwardly with the discomfort. So why do we do it? Part of the answer comes from all the lectures that were given to us "to teach us a lesson." Such an approach is habitual and automatic, a reaction rather than an intentional response. Lecturing also prevails when we are frustrated and do not know, or do not use, other tools to communicate. We tend to lecture children because we are disappointed with them, and want them to improve. Perhaps our disappointment with kids reflects our disappointment with ourselves. Lecturing can be a way of displacing our personal letdowns on to children.

When receiving a lecture, the child feels helpless and out of control. Ironically, so does the adult issuing the lecture. Beneath the commanding exterior, the adult does not really know what to do with the child's problem, so he delivers tirades to drown out the problem... and the child.

When we talk to a young person, remember that there is an individual on the receiving end of our words. A telltale sign of lecturing is getting so swept away by what we say that the listener is forgotten.

For children, the downpour of our words produces defense mechanisms. Just as we did during childhood, children must shelter themselves when adults speak too harshly and critically to them. They defend themselves by tuning us out to soften the blow of our words. Or maybe they fight back with arguments and impulsive defenses.

We remember intense experiences, such as someone yelling at us. But, unfortunately, what we remember is not that we committed a mistake, but how bad we are. And that does not teach us to learn and grow and be genuinely remorseful.

Take a deep breath now. Remember what we explored in Part 2 of this book, "Getting to the Basics." Remember about listening to kids. Remember about sharing our own feelings so children can become aware of theirs. Remember that there are better ways to express our anger, frustration, and disappointment with children than to lecture them. Remember about taking responsibility for the way we communicate and solve problems, so we can teach kids how to become more responsible. Remember about learning from our mistakes.

Other Considerations

To be sure, there are times when words of caution, warning, and correction are needed. But such serious messages need not be delivered as a lecture, resulting in an attack on a child's character. Instead of saying "You're a thief and a liar! Do you want to end up in prison?" you can say, "I am disappointed and disturbed to find out you were stealing and lied about what you did. Where do you think this behavior will lead you? Let's look at what happened, and what can now be done to set things straight."

In addition to understanding the impact of lecturing, there are two other important considerations: finding alternatives to lecturing, and forgiving oneself and others for their part in talks that belittle kids.

Many of the tools in this volume will naturally diminish lecturing and provide healthy alternatives. Another option for effective communication is a five-step problem-solving process that is detailed in my previous book, *Getting Thru to Kids: Problem Solving with Children Ages 6 to 18*. It identifies the problem, explores feelings about the problem, discovers negative beliefs, finds new outlooks, and then visualizes a different future.

Positive And Negative Cycles

The negative lecturing cycle starts with a child's problem, which disturbs the adult. Here is how the cycle continues for the adult's part: The adult is initially disturbed by the child's problem; and then reacts with confusion, thinking she should know how to handle the child. She becomes frustrated that she is at a loss on what to do. She decides to lecture the youngster so the situation will go away. But it doesn't. Instead of dealing with the problem it worsens. Both adult and child end up disempowered.

An alternative positive cycle that avoids lecturing starts off the same: The child has a problem, which disturbs the adult. But instead of lecturing, the adult appropriately expresses her feelings to the child. Then she helps the young person understand and, if appropriate, resolve the situation. Remember, the more a child can solve his own problems, the better. The adult judiciously helps the child, instead of trying to rescue him. Thus both adult and child are empowered. Table 10 illustrates both cycles.

TABLE 10
ALTERNATIVE RESPONSES TO A CHILD'S PROBLEM

Adult's Negative Cycle	Adult's Positive Cycle
Feels disturbed by child's problem	Feels disturbed by child's problem
Thinks "should" know how to handle it	Reflects and allows talk to unfold
Frustrated, at a loss	Appropriately expresses feelings
Lectures and situation worsens	Helps child understand and resolve situation
Adult and child disempowered	Adult and child empowered

★ TOOL 12 ★
Phrases and Tips to Avoid Lecturing

Liberate yourself and your kids from sermonizing and lecturing. As an antidote to such one-sided talks, remember to include the listener. Use *phrases* such as:

- "Have you ever thought of..."
- "You may already be aware that..."
- "You may have heard of this before..."

Remember these *tips* to help avoid lecturing:

- Monitor your nonverbal language: tone, posture, and voice level. Are you finger-pointing and yelling, or keeping your posture erect with a firm tone of voice?

- Share your own feelings and elicit the child's feelings. "I feel hurt and disappointed when you..."

- Explore thoughts and beliefs about the situation. "It seems you acted that way because you thought things were unfair."

- Seek alternative solutions and behaviors. "Instead of kicking the chair, what else could you have done?"

- Reflect on the consequences of the situation. "You will need to go without your..."

- Include the listener's experience and understanding when you speak. This act of including the person validates him or her. "I know you think it's unfair when your sister gets to play with the toys for so long."

ALLOWING FOR THE SILENCES

A Hebrew sage said, "The beginning of wisdom is silence; the second stage is listening." How, then, do we allow for the silence so our wisdom will grow?

Some of the silence will come from shifting communication patterns as we provide children with more opportunity for self-expression. It means we will say less, and kids will say more. At first children may resist talking, uncertain that they actually have the chance to talk more.

There will be awkward silences too. Especially when discussing important topics or problems, there needs to be time for processing. Youth, with their lack of both experience and conceptual thinking, may sometimes be slower to process than adults. But even adults need quiet, reflective time for answers to bubble up from their consciousness.

Initially, the silences will probably be more uncomfortable for us than for the kids. The children will just be reflecting, while we may be worried about not knowing what to say. Allowing children more freedom to feel, think, and respond, we are free from the burden of having to know all the answers...and it may take some time adjusting to this approach.

Remember that we often talk as a filler, as a way of preventing true communication from occurring. As we allow for silences, we can also allow ourselves not to have immediate answers. In what seems like an empty void, there are vast, untapped resources available to both us and children. Just *be there* with kids, while they develop their own responses. Silently co-existing with young people is a profound experience. Children then are wonderfully supported and guided in a wordless environment. After some practice, we learn to savor these periods of silence with their deeply felt communication.

> *Silence provides both security and the freedom to discover new possibilities.*

The key is in *how* we interact with kids. It is not only just what we say; communication also includes what occurs between the words, allowing time to just be, to digest, and to reflect in silence. Just as between each inhale and exhale we breathe there exists a pause, so too can we acknowledge the silences between speaking. We can practice allowing for the silences today, and see how it deepens our relationships with children.

ACCEPTING, LETTING GO, AND LEARNING

This chapter is not intended to make us feel guilty, blaming ourselves for past lectures and ramblings. Thinking about excessive and ill-chosen words we have used with kids may, upon reflection, cause us some discomfort. However, we can acknowledge our past miscommunication, realizing that we can learn from the experiences. Let's use our experiences, challenging ourselves to create alternative ways to communicate with kids in the future.

Who among us has not lectured a child, just as we were lectured to when growing up? Who has not rambled on amid the glazed looks and deaf ears of kids? Recognizing that we were carried away with our words should not be an excuse for self-pity. Let it be a source of genuine remorse, a subject that is dealt with in the next two chapters. It is an opportunity for another growth choice, and a chance to find a better means for self-expression.

Armed with tools for encouraging children to answer, we can promote listening, question-asking, and evenhanded limit-setting. We can also listen more to the silences, which will offer us unexpected gifts and resources. Our growing repertoire of communication approaches allows everyone to feel more respect and dignity, which in turn creates better questions and truer answers.

Let's add to our repertoire by seeing how we can turn our mistakes into opportunities.

CHAPTER ELEVEN

Learning From Our Mistakes

Children are just like adults in that we all have the opportunity to grow and explore the human experience. Part of that experience is making "mistakes"...which we are supposed to learn from. Right?

Too often children see their elders blaming, denying, and excusing instead of owning up to mistakes. Here are a couple of questions to consider:

- When was the last time you admitted a mistake to yourself?

- When was the last time you admitted a mistake to children in your life?

Even though kids may ignore and resist us, they do pay attention to our actions and note inconsistencies and errors. We know they will point them out to us. When a young person calls attention to our own mistakes, we have some choices on how to respond:

1. Ignore the child's comments.

2. Discount our error ("Oh, it doesn't matter," or "I didn't mean it," or "Don't worry about it").

3. Point out how the child makes mistakes too.

4. Thank the child for helping point out our error so we can improve.

From these choices, answer number 4 offers the best opportunity to learn from mistakes; yet often we do not gracefully acknowledge children for their feedback. Children try to legitimately help us when we fall, just as we try to help them. In fact, they learned from us how to help and correct others. They are also interested in seeing how we handle ourselves when we are down. Do we follow the advice we give them?

To prepare ourselves for the mistakes we will make, it helps to develop positive beliefs. Examples of positive life-enhancing beliefs are "I can improve" and "I learn from my mistakes." These outlooks uplift child and adult alike.

Children grow more secure knowing
we can handle errors and solve problems.
Our openness then strengthens our ability
to guide, nurture, and educate kids.

We don't need to be infallible people, knowing all the answers. When we cover up our own errors, we end up justifying our behavior to kids. Instead, we can see our mistakes as feedback on areas that call for improvement.

★ TOOL 13 ★
Learning From Your Mistakes

Here is a way to examine how you handle mistakes. In this exercise, mistakes are used as learning experiences. This process applies to both adults and children. Feel free to write down your responses.

1. Remember the last time you made a mistake. Describe what occurred, including your response to others. What did you say to yourself or others about your error?

2. If you did try to cover up or ignore your error, how could you have handled it differently? What can you learn from the mistake, however big or small it was? If you did handle the error with an honest admission, congratulate yourself. What did you learn from the situation?

3. Set a goal for yourself of observing the next time you make a mistake. What approach will you take? How can you make it a learning experience?

When we acknowledge mistakes, a learning process begins. We can find areas that need the tonic of healthy remorse. We can also recognize that mistakes are part of our experience, rather than considering ourselves as a mistake. Learning from feedback is crucial for everyone. In a spirit of growth, we cultivate an attitude of being open to feedback. We then can evaluate what there is to learn in certain situations. The trick is to avoid the extremes of either ignoring our errors or becoming overwhelmed by the feedback we receive. In other words, just as we want to pay attention to our mistakes, we also don't want to become paralyzed by dwelling on what happens to us.

Strangely enough, though, we often forget that it is easier to learn how to improve in areas where we falter, as opposed to repeating our errors and creating the same stressful results.

Life is too short to keep covering up our shortcomings.

Youth will continue to test us to see if our concern and guidance is heartfelt. Kids will point out, sometimes in blunt ways, wherever we are incomplete within ourselves. Our self-deception and our own immaturity inevitably surface like an unsightly blemish. And children in our care will quickly notice what is wrong and make their comments, however directly or indirectly. By attending to our weaknesses and ignorance, we gain strength. Our inner knowing then translates outwardly to communicating and teaching others. As we learn how to guide ourselves, we can guide the children in our care. They want to know we care for them, and that we will provide the help they need to mature.

USING OPPORTUNITIES

When kids point out our shortcomings, it is an opportunity—for us and for them. We can be in denial and resort to authoritarian tactics. Or we can discuss the children's observations. Sometimes we can gracefully thank them for their feedback.

Sometimes we can teach them more socially acceptable ways to communicate: "John, instead of saying this history lesson is stupid, there is another way you can say it. I appreciate the feedback. But I can hear it better, and you'd be a better communicator, if you said something like 'Can't we do something different today? Maybe write a short story about George Washington instead of reading from the book again."

I sometimes ask my students if I should get mad when they correct me. For example, if they point out a spelling error I made on the board, I tell them, "Should I start yelling at you for correcting me? How about if I blame you for mistakes you made? How about if I throw my marker on the floor?" I sometimes raise my voice in a mock-attempt to display anger. My students seem to enjoy when I playfully show them inappropriate ways to deal with my own mistakes.

Children welcome it when we admit that we don't know something, acknowledging that we too struggle to understand things. Like fresh air, our honesty comes as a relief to kids. They are liberated, no longer dependent on the all-knowing adult. Children then become freer to learn from their mistakes and grow as well.

Adults' openness is inspirational to everyone. It reminds us that we are human, with an extraordinary range of thoughts, feelings, and experiences. We are all learning and growing on this mysterious planet within a vast universe. Such awareness can take communication to a whole new level and bring wonderful results.

This chapter focused primarily on how we teach kids about handling mistakes by using ourselves as an example. We become powerful role models to children when we recognize our errors as they occur in the moment. We can also realize that if we ignore our shortcomings and let kids call them to our attention, it may be more embarrassing than if we correct ourselves.

Now that we can deal with our own mistakes, let's see how we can help kids use remorse in response to their errors.

CHAPTER TWELVE

Helping Kids with Remorse

I recently tried to locate a certain book and called several bookstores. Unintentionally, I called the same store twice and ended up speaking with the same manager I had called the previous day. Once I realized I had repeated my request to the same person, it was too late. The manager had already begun a mild reprimand, telling me he was quite busy and didn't have time for me to call him daily about my book order. Embarrassed, I apologized: "I'm sorry, I didn't mean to disturb you. I got mixed up."

In that situation, I experienced remorse for my action because I had unnecessarily taken up another person's time and energy. Alternatively, I could have tried to cover up my error, making excuses for my behavior, perhaps even retaliating with rude remarks. Or an equally ineffective response would have been making an insincere apology, saying something in the hopes the manager would more quickly dismiss my error.

DISTINGUISHING RIGHT FROM WRONG

The Longman Dictionary tells us remorse means "sorrow for having done wrong." Although remorse can be uncomfortable, it enhances our awareness. Such awareness increases our choices, some of which include correcting errors, building strength, and fulfilling one's potential through life. Remorse then equates to "healthy shame."

Instead of remorse, when we have done something wrong, we can respond with despair and hopelessness, which leads to self-pity and depression. Hopelessness and despair turn us against ourselves, believing that we are defective and flawed. These emotions equate with "unhealthy shame."

For example, if the child breaks grandmother's vase, he can feel like a horrible person, who is forever banned from the premises (unhealthy shame). Or he can feel sorry that he was careless (healthy shame). In unhealthy shame, the person criticizes himself and just feels worse. In healthy shame, the person criticizes his actions so he can learn and improve.

Validate children's self-worth while helping them evoke remorse for their errors.

Use a neutral, sometimes concerned tone, a language that is free of moralizing and judging. The child then knows that you are acting out of care. You may need to disapprove of the act while still approving of the person. This approach creates security and room for the young person to improve. "Susie, when you steal things, I get very concerned. You know it's wrong, and that I disapprove. How do you feel after taking that? What do you plan to do now?"

Feeling remorse is the feedback we need to correct our errors. If we did not feel some regret for our errors, we would continue to keep making them without indications that a problem exists. On a physical level, if we did not feel pain when we cut ourselves, we might not realize we need to care for the wound. On an emotional and intellectual level, the inner disturbance of our conscience reminds us of what needs to be healed.

RESPONDING WITH REMORSE AFTER THE MISTAKE

The last chapter covered how adults' responses to mistakes can serve as a model. This chapter focuses on how to help children have remorse as direct feedback for their growth. To understand the value of remorse, explore with young people what can happen after they make a mistake. Consider these three possible choices:

- Covering up the error.
- Making an insincere apology.
- Expressing sincere regret over their actions.

Covering up the error: In discussions with teenagers, I hear them conclude that the more you cover up, the bigger the problem gets. Teens can more readily come to this conclusion on their own if we don't preach to them about being honest. They further note that covering up makes you untrustworthy and viewed as a manipulator. Hiding mistakes can also become a bad habit. Such an approach creates two problems for the person who conceals the truth: the original wrongdoing and the lie that covers it up.

Making an insincere apology: Sometimes a child says what you want to hear as a way to avoid unpleasant consequences. In discussing this approach with him, the young person might say he feels powerful by "getting away" with his actions and deceiving others. But as you explore further, and ask what is underneath those feelings of power, the child reveals feelings of fear and weakness. The child's "solutions" that involve manipulation stem from the distrust of self and others. These dishonest approaches are only temporary fixes that can come unglued at any time. When the true nature of the mistake or the insincere apology comes to light, each party ends up distrusting the other.

Expressing sincere regret over their actions: The third choice for dealing with mistakes is to honestly admit the error and express sincere regret. By careful listening, questioning, and exploring consequences, you can help young people come to this place of remorse for their own misdeeds. Remorse entails regret for one's actions, accounting for the situation, and taking responsibility for any damage—all of which teaches deep lessons and moral development. You may need to confront children, but remember that this is an opportunity for profound learning, not a time to assault their character.

We all make mistakes; remorse puts us in
touch with the thoughts and feelings that let
us learn from those experiences.

By neutrally presenting to children the three options of handling mistakes—covering up errors, making an insincere apology, and expressing sincere regret—kids will often make the best choice.

If they resist taking responsibility and experiencing remorse for mistakes, give them time to think about your discussion concerning what they did. Then you can return to the subject at an time. Also, examine your own approach for any moralizing that may have created unhealthy shame and hampered communication with the children.

Helping kids with remorse centers on acknowledging them as people, while addressing certain errors that have been committed. Ask them how others were affected by their actions. Discuss in a neutral way how they would feel if the misdeeds were done to them. Possibly they have repeated a transgression that was done to them. Explain, then, how negative cycles occur when people keep exchanging unpleasant actions toward each other. If they keep repeating the same mistakes, how will that affect their family, classroom, and community? To conclude, reassure them of their own value.

AN ILLUSTRATION

Here is how I encouraged one student to be remorseful:

> During one of my classes, fifteen-year-old Sam proudly said he wanted to be a marine biologist. Jay, one of his peers, suddenly called out, "Sure! Are you kidding? You don't know what you're talking about." Sam's face flushed as he squirmed in his chair.
>
> I later questioned Jay as to why he was so demeaning toward Sam. He explained that he thought Sam was pipe-dreaming, that given his academic ability becoming a marine biologist was impossible.
>
> I asked Jay if anyone had ever questioned him about *his* ability.
>
> "Sure. People used to tell me I couldn't do well in school."
>
> "How did you feel about that?"

"Upset and angry."

"Sounds like that was hurtful too," I added, to empathize with his situation. "So I know you don't think Sam could become a marine biologist. But should you put him down, especially in front of his peers?"

"I guess not. I could just talk to him in private or keep quiet about it."

"Is it okay for you to make mistakes?"

"Yeah, I guess so."

"Is it okay if Sam wants to be a marine biologist even if he doesn't end up being one?"

"Yeah."

"Jay, I know you can do the positive thing, even if you make a mistake."

Jay nodded.

This illustration shows how by questioning and empathizing you can naturally elicit remorse from children. Then once they have released their feelings through remorse, you can help guide them to other appropriate ways to express thoughts and feelings.

Remorse teaches us that all roads can lead back to the truth. And this is how we heal and grow.

NURTURING THE CONSCIENCE

We all know that "little voice inside," the trustworthy guide that helps us make the right choices. That inner guide can be our best friend or a distant stranger, depending on how we treat it.

Young children can be quick to tell you right from wrong. As they grow, the complications grow too. Living in a world that extends beyond their families can create a moral questioning as their awareness expands. Yet that little voice doesn't dim amid the growing awareness of the world's complexity.

Conscience keeps us honest and helps us create healthy boundaries.

Conscience can be a powerful guide, if we allow it to be heard. On the other hand, the more lies and deception occur, the more conscience recedes, clouded over by an inability to act with appropriate shame. It is a matter of listening to the inner intelligence. Instruct kids to heed their own conscience, and show them how this self-awareness helps them meet their needs in a healthy way.

The goal, then, is to help children understand how to make good choices, ones that can help them and others the best they know how. For younger children, right and wrong can be quite clear-cut, an either/or choice, a yes or no. As they age, other considerations—peer relations, curiosity, independence—come into play. Learning from experiences, the person more reliably knows how to steer through many situations, knowing what is right for herself or himself.

Such a progression allows a person to pass through the stages of childhood development. This moral development propels one to grow spiritually, gathering individual experiences and integrating them into his or her personal awareness. A person then becomes more of an individual, and can contribute more to society. The person is also better prepared to fulfill his or her life's purpose. The conscience serves as an invaluable resource, a light shining through the confusion of everyday life.

★ TOOL 14 ★
Affirmations For Healthy Remorse

Here is a set of affirmations that can be used with adults as well as children. The sayings can be adapted to fit the person's particular age and situation. Use them in discussions and problem-solving with kids. Also be open to finding other outlets for bringing these powerful statements to fruition. Remorse leads to self-acceptance and fulfilling one's life potential; helping children with this powerful emotion thus deserves our time and attention. The following concepts will create a foundation to develop character and freedom in children.

- I can make mistakes. I can still be okay, regardless of what I did.

- I can forgive myself and let others forgive me.

- I can flow with change, whether I am prepared or not.

- I can get my needs and desires met. I can allow for others' needs and desires as well.

- I can grow.

These affirmations tell the child that perfection is not the goal. Rather, living and learning is what counts. Everyone is forgivable. Change is a part of life; allow the river to flow. Everyone has needs and desires that can be met, including the child. One is free to grow, not merely out of duty and obligation, but by personal choice for self-expression. In these ways, the young person can naturally experience sorrow, feeling genuinely sorry rather than experiencing self-pity.

By your intent and assistance, you can help the child internalize such life-affirming statements. These concepts then act as stepping stones for the young person's character development.

★ TOOL 15 ★
Acting as an Honorable Person

The following tool helps children see their mistakes as a way of connecting with their goodness, rather than reinforcing their feelings of being bad and defective. When an incident connects with children's (or adults') unresolved issues, they become shame-based, seeing the error as another example of how terrible they are. By contrast, as already outlined, healthy shame creates remorse for mistakes, a way to learn and grow from our experiences.

This tool has two parts:

1. Identify the error the young person committed.

2. Ask "How would a good [or honorable] person deal with this mistake?"

The word "honorable" may take some explaining, which can stimulate some thought-provoking discussion. You can also choose other comparable words besides "good" or "honorable," such as "respectable" or "trustworthy," to describe a person who learns from mistakes, rather than defending the error.

This powerful approach gives the young person a way to save face, that is, to avoid being consumed by negative shame.

It creates a structure to allow for the healthy cleansing of remorse. The child can then experience embarrassment or regret for actions and make amends to the people affected. For example, if a youngster takes another's toy, she can return it with an apology. If a student calls out in class, he can promise to raise his hand next time and perhaps apologize for disrupting the class. Kids can then act honorably, doing the right thing from their hearts, not because someone makes them do it.

This tool also offers a way to develop the positive belief that a student once expressed to me. We had discussed the impact of his misbehavior, and he concisely concluded: "After I make a mistake, I can make up for it."

The "honorable person" approach is more comprehensive than the adult simply offering corrections, identifying a positive behavior to replace the negative behavior. To be sure, positive corrections are instructive; constructive feedback could include, "You know to respect others' things," or "Raise your hand before speaking." But the "honorable person" tool takes the learning an important step further: It *first* helps children to experience the discomfort of their misconduct, and then they can find a way to set things straight. In other words, you communicate more than "You need to be friendlier," or "You need to follow the rules better." You help kids realize that their inappropriate words and actions affect others and should cause them some remorse.

This approach makes it easier for the young people to understand and process their errors.

You assist children by validating their self-worth while dealing with the problem at hand. You support kids, without rescuing them. You help them recognize the shortcomings of covering up errors and making insincere apologies. Children then have room to internally shift their responses from being shame-based to truly remorseful, which helps them feel good about themselves. Although children should be ashamed of certain mistakes, we can continually teach them to be proud of themselves.

LEARNING AS WE GO

As you progress through your journey, you can share your own successes and failures with kids, doing so in a way that will help them learn and grow. Children must traverse their own paths, make their mistakes, ignoring and realigning with their own consciences. Thus we all go our separate ways, yet continue to come together as we share our mistakes, becoming that much wiser in the process. Just as much of our growth comes from our successes, so do our mistakes offer invaluable opportunities for self-development.

To balance helping children experience remorse, let's look next at how to help children value honesty. By promoting kids' honesty, we also reduce the times they must experience remorse because of their dishonesty.

CHAPTER THIRTEEN

Developing Honesty

One of the challenges of helping kids with remorse and other positive qualities is our dualistic view of honesty. We value honesty, yet we often give incentives for dishonesty. It can be easy to be less than honest.

For instance, it often appears to be fine for a person to falsely accuse another and take her to court. The problem is that the accuser has no accountability, whereas the accused could be honest and have to risk reputation and finances to defend herself against a dishonest accuser who can walk away from the trial with no losses and possible gains from a dishonest claim.

How many times do individuals and insurance companies make dishonest claims to reduce and avoid settlements?

Investors, like many CEOs, often have a single-minded goal: to make money, regardless of how it affects others or the environment.

In politics, how many politicians have maligned their opponents? Too often elections favor the politician who has the most negative campaign.

Children notice these kinds of behaviors and how their fallout affects the world around them. The message becomes: It's good to be honest, but there are times when it's inconvenient. In fact, bending the truth can be to your advantage.

For children, this perspective can translate into a belief that "lying gets you out of trouble." Why do kids lie? Children know they have committed an error—such as stealing or unfriendliness—and may want to cover it up and avoid punishment. If the punishment is abuse, such as tirades and beatings, it is understandable that children will lie. Also, as mentioned in the above examples, they may get the impression that there is much to gain from dishonesty.

Very young children can innocently confuse fantasy with reality. At that stage, you can gently help kids understand how wishing and actuality are often different. You can still encourage their imagination in play, stories, and fantasy.

As children age, lying can become a way of avoiding responsibility. Some young people's ability to lie can become so polished that it is difficult to detect. Eventually the lying is discovered and consequences are meted out. Without careful feedback and guidance, the young person may still figure he can beat the odds and gain more from dishonesty than honesty. Also, if he receives too severe a consequence, too punishing a response, he may become more hardened in his deceit.

The goal is for everyone to value honesty even if it comes in the form of admitting misconduct. After an admission, let us beware about merely scolding children for their mistakes without putting value on when they honestly admit their errors. Such an approach may inadvertently encourage them to lie so as to avoid unpleasant consequences. It is easy to tell the truth when we did the right thing; it is much harder when we know we have erred. Then we must deal with our own self-criticism in addition to that of others.

We need to make sure children realize that truth-telling has incentives.

Appreciating children for telling the truth, especially at those difficult confessional moments, goes a long way toward establishing trust and healthy remorse with young people. It also helps children develop the character to be honest in the future.

HANDLING DISHONESTY

The reason people often lie is to defend against an error in judgment they have made. The lie compounds the problem: Now there is the lie in addition to the original error. When kids lie, it can be confusing for adults to deal with dishonesty, because so much is occurring at once.

To treat the double whammy of a lie and its underlying problem, start by addressing the dishonesty in order to discover what actually happened. Nonetheless, you still need to deal with the underlying problem. For example, you can say, "I appreciate your honesty in telling me you took the cookies. Now we need to find out what was going on there." Following through in the situation will probably involve some consequence, connecting the child's behaviors with particular results (see Chapter 15).

Children come to realize that certain actions bring unpleasant results. This feedback is how they learn. Even if a lie might help evade the consequences, kids need to understand that covering up their actions by lying compounds the problem. How do you help children realize that lying makes a situation worse instead of it being a convenient way to avoid trouble? Explain that lying leads to "living a lie": After telling a lie, the person must maintain his false account. He is thus kept on guard and separate from others. This drains energy, undermines trust, and lowers self-esteem.

Lying usually links with other problems, which only adds to the trouble children experience. Dishonesty can also easily become a defense mechanism and a bad habit. Help kids to realize that telling the truth may be difficult at times, but it offers great benefits: It eliminates additional negative consequences while building trust and character.

★ TOOL 16 ★
Honesty and Its Benefits

What can you do to untie a lie and its tangled web? Here are two tools to help a child become more honest. The first approach helps clean up dishonesty; the second tool reinforces children for telling the truth. Both methods help children get in the practice of truth-telling.

For this first tool, start by asking the young person a series of questions after learning that he or she was dishonest. Focus on the consequences of honesty and dishonesty, so the child can see where each will lead.

- First, discuss the consequences of believing that "lying gets you out of trouble."

- Be nonjudgmental and neutral in your discussion.

- Ask, "What will happen if you keep lying?" The answer will probably be, "I'll get caught." You might add that being "caught" has already happened or you wouldn't be having this discussion with the child. Then ask with sincerity, "Do you like being caught?" and "How does that feel?"

- After exploring the discomforts of being caught, you can ask the child for alternatives to the "lying gets you out of trouble" approach. Usually a more positive belief like "I can be more honest" or "I can tell the truth" will emerge.

- Ask the child about the consequences of being more honest. Relate it to developing trust and maturity.

- Congratulate the young person for coming to that conclusion for himself or herself.

Just keep summarizing and asking questions until children realize the truth for themselves. You are a guide, fact-finder, and facilitator in the process. The lying may need direct consequences as well, such as a loss of certain privileges because of how the child's actions undermined trust. As children realize the value of being more honest, you can encourage them to rebuild trust and regain privileges.

★ TOOL 17 ★
Catch Children Being Honest

"Thanks for telling me about how you played in the game. It's nice that you are honest about what is happening with you." This is an example of the second remedy for dishonesty, designed to help children establish a pattern of honesty. You can start by acknowledging even incidental remarks that show an honest account of any behavior they have done, whether their actions were appropriate or inappropriate. Remember, the aim is to promote honest responses.

Here is another example, illustrating both an appropriate and inappropriate action by the child, while still commending the youngster for honesty in either case. "Thank you for telling me you put the food back in the refrigerator. It was honest of you to tell me, and it also was helpful." Or "Thank you for telling me you forgot to put the food back in the refrigerator. I'm sorry you forgot, and next time I hope you'll remember. But you were honest for telling me about it when I asked."

You can value that a child told you about mundane things, like how much TV he watched or what game she played. Then kids will come to expect that you value truthful responses when more uncomfortable matters occur.

The challenge may come when they misbehave. In order to make sure you know what happened, ask children about what they did *after* you have already observed them. In other words, you already know the truth; you are just checking to see if they answer truthfully. As previously mentioned, you can begin checking on routine things that are done appropriately by the child. "Joe, did you close the door when you came in?"

"Yes."

"Thanks for being honest."

Then shift from a positive behavior to checking a misbehavior that you observed. "Joe, were you just unfriendly to your sister?"

"Well...yes."

"Thanks for being honest. Now let's talk about calling her names."

After a while, children will expect that you probably know what they did, so they habitually tell you the truth. It also helps you when you don't know what actually happened, because the child assumes you do and tells you the truth.

This approach runs counter to the way we usually deal with children. Normally, children figure we ask them what happened because we *don't* know what actually occurred when they erred. Kids are sometimes tempted to bend the truth lest they receive a scolding and unpleasant consequences. We also forget to value them for telling the truth after an error; instead, we just focus on the problem and all the trouble it has caused. Conversely, the catch-kids-being-honest approach values them for their honesty while still holding them accountable for their behavior. It respects kids for their truthful responses, which creates an incentive for honesty.

You might wonder whether this process, asking kids if they did something when you already know the answer, is manipulative and dishonest in itself. Remember that this approach aims to help improve children's honesty, which is accomplished by our care and guidance. It is akin to asking children an academic question to which you already know the answer. You ask as a way of teaching, caring, and connecting with children.

By your valuing children's honesty, even in small matters, they become personally accountable. Children learn to recognize their behavior and take responsibility for it.

Here then is a summary of the catching-kids-being-honest approach:

1. First ask the child about some action she did that you have already observed. The action can be routine and appropriate, such as sitting in a chair.

2. Thank her for honestly telling you what she did.

3. Then shift to asking her whether she did something inappropriate, such as taking another's comic book without permission. Regardless of whether you observed her action, the child will expect that she has been observed and will tell you the truth, even if her action was inappropriate.

When catching kids being honest, just remember to keep telling them how much you value their honesty in spite of how much they misbehaved. This approach can be a discipline in tolerance and acceptance on your part as well. As discussed in Chapter 15, children's misconduct needs to be directly addressed by you with suitable responses and consequences. But by being recognized for their honesty, children will experience significant gains in self-esteem. And self-esteem is the way they evaluate themselves.

Both techniques for developing honesty—asking questions and reinforcing honest responses—work well alone or together. Keep catching children being honest and reinforcing the belief that "I tell the truth." That will improve the chances of the next generation living in a world where people are much more honest with each other.

Next let's look at another area where children experience misunderstanding; namely, how to understand the relationship between courage and risk-taking.

CHAPTER FOURTEEN

Understanding Courage and Risk-Taking

Courage may often be simpler and more commonplace than we realize. Winston Churchill summarized it as follows: "Courage is what it takes to stand up and speak. Courage is also what it takes to sit down and listen." This description suggests that there are many opportunities to act courageously for both young and old alike.

Courage can be a wonderful, enhancing part of life. It gives us an opportunity to prove ourselves to those we live with, and ultimately to ourselves.

Let's look closer at the quality of courage. Children start at a young age to understand how heroes and heroines in stories display bravery in the face of challenging circumstances. By the time adolescence arrives, however, youth can confuse risk-taking with courage. Statistics in the United States show that from ages 10 to 24, many young people practice such risky behaviors as drinking and driving, driving without seat belts, and carrying weapons to school. As of 1997, adolescents account for half of the 40,000 people diagnosed each year with HIV. Three million get sexually transmitted diseases annually. One million become pregnant.

The confusion lies in the fact that courage requires risk-taking, but risk-taking is not necessarily courageous. Kids can mistakenly identify courage as taking drugs, walking on thin ice, and driving far above the speed limit. Although dangerous and thrilling, those risks do not translate into courage.

The key qualification for courage is determining whether your action helps yourself or others. Discovering how much alcohol you can drink does not help anyone; actually, it can be harmful and destructive.

OPPORTUNITIES FOR COURAGE

Opportunities for courage come on many fronts for children. Sports help kids to develop courage, meeting challenges through competition and overcoming their own perceived limitations. Also, there are times when kids assist someone who is in need, sometimes in a situation of immediate danger. Examples of this kind of courage include a child helping a family member who was injured, or a youngster saving a sibling who was in danger of drowning. Another example of courage can occur when adolescents go AWOL from a treatment program, running away from their issues, and then deciding to return to the facility.

Perhaps the most available, yet overlooked, opportunities for courage come in dealing with our own weaknesses, the kind of obstacles in development that we have been exploring throughout this book. Being vulnerable to others, selectively sharing with others those areas where we experience difficulty, can involve a risk. In addition, communicating feelings involves a risk of exposing ourselves in a way that can be misused by others.

Yet as the saying goes, as we become most personal, we become most universal. We get real by leveling with others, so we can feel, think, and validate our lives. It can also take bravery to be honest in the face of tough consequences. To summon courage, we may need to admit transgressions and poor choices, knowing that taking responsibilities for our actions can sometimes be bitter medicine.

True courage takes us into the unknown, where our potential lies. We can help ourselves self-actualize, fulfilling our growth stages by embracing courage. A toddler may need courage to walk; a grade-schooler needs courage to enter school; an adolescent needs courage to be responsible with his or her body; and the adult may need courage to find a job that is fulfilling. Each stage of development interacts with and affects the later stages. Children may have mastered learning how to walk, but there are continual new tasks and adventures where they need to risk falling in order to grow. It could be starting a new hobby or learning more about the computer. It takes courage to risk those falls so we can continue to rise and climb throughout life. These efforts fulfill the mind, body, and spirit.

DOES IT HELP?

It is wise to keep in mind that a certain amount of thrill-seeking accompanies growing up.

Thrills, such as skateboarding or going on a roller coaster ride, can be enjoyable when they don't put the person or others at undue risk. Children are curious, wanting to experiment, sometimes to assert their independence, and to test society's limits. In those thrills, kids find their passion, which they can ultimately learn to follow for their life's purpose. But during adolescence, children live in a world of violence, substance abuse, sexually transmitted diseases, and unintended pregnancies that we know can make it a dangerous time to experiment.

The key goes back to determining what is helpful. Stealing for a friend is risky, and whom does it help? Is it worth the risk? Asking for help on a school paper can be a risk too, but it clearly can bring helpful results. Controlling your temper can take some courage as well.

Let's help ourselves and our kids find acts of courage in daily life, however seemingly small or slight. Let's also determine when courage becomes too risky, too dangerous. Let's seek courage in unrecognized places, such as admitting a mistake. When we recognize and celebrate courage, we help kids—and adults—grow and feel good about themselves.

★ TOOL 18 ★
Exploring Courage

To help clarify courage, you and your children can complete the following series of sentences. This inventory was drawn in part from Laura Davis' *Courage to Heal Workbook.*

- Courage is...

- Who is someone I know (personally or I heard about) who has shown courage? Describe those acts of courage.

- When have I been courageous? How did I demonstrate courage? (You can include facing fears, sharing feelings, and helping someone that took a risk of any degree.) Whom did it help, including myself? If no personal courage comes to mind, could I ever do something courageous? Explain.

- I lost courage when...

- I've taken risks that weren't courageous (helpful to myself or others) when I...

- In the future, I can be more courageous by...

THE COURAGEOUS FOOL

Another way to understand courage is by examining the image of the fool. The fool can be seen as an archetype, a universal image that we draw on and follow in our lives. Like other archetypes, such as the orphan, the lover, the warrior, and the magician, the fool offers a way to understand the positive and negative traits that influence us.

The negative aspect of the fool has him taking "foolhardy risks," jumping off a cliff, hurling into a meaningless oblivion. Also, the fool can be a slave to his own whims and impulses, consumed by recklessness and selfishness.

The positive side of the fool provides us some further insights into courage. Think of the court jester, with his comical and delightful garb, entertaining and criticizing rulers. The jester speaks the truth in a straightforward way that others would not conceive of, much less speak.

When you and your kids become the courageous fool, you follow the unknown, trusting your intuition, knowing that some things cannot be explained. You understand that life transcends reason and convention, yet the unknown must still be followed to heed some inner call for self-fulfillment. For an adult, this might mean leaving a job, or moving to another home. For a child, this might mean trying a new game or food, or going to meet new kids. Such courage can require trust, following those gut feelings that can lead us around the corner to encounter what we cannot see, but know we must meet for inexplicable reasons.

An example of playing the fool is the class clown. The negative class clown uses humor to disrupt, ridicule, and embarrass. In contrast, the positive class clown takes the high road, using humor to relieve tension, finding appropriate ways to lighten up the environment. The positive clown becomes a wonderful teacher using unorthodox methods. The negative class clown expresses fear, whereas the positive class clown expresses love.

Considered to be "foolish," artists, inventors, and innovators are often met with criticism and resistance. Yet without that archetypal fool within us all, we would lead quite a drab, stagnant life. We would be deprived of the rich experiences and fulfilling mysteries that courage brings, prompted by our intuition.

We can play the selfish and hurtful fool, the one who indulges in vanity, apathy, and carelessness. Or we can teach ourselves and our children to play the positive fool, the one who has humor, detachment, and creativity.

★ TOOL 19 ★
Courage to Play the Fool

To gain understanding and wisdom about how to play the fool, use the following exercise:

1. Think of examples where you played the negative and the positive fool. For the negative fool, identify rash and impulsive behavior. For the positive fool, identify risking something to benefit yourself or another.

2. Identify and imagine how you might play the negative and positive fool in the future.

3. Create a dialog with the positive fool. Take the risk to try this dialogue, and let the fool offer you advice. Sometimes routines and habits need to be broken so you can experience more of life. Let the fool lead you to wholeness, to a fearlessness that can help you and others, in spite of what anyone thinks.

Understanding courage requires discrimination. We can help kids know when to act and when to refrain, to distinguish the uplifting thrills from the destructive ones. When children connect with their hearts and minds, they gather the love and wisdom to be courageous.

To continue developing this part of the book, "Making Growth Choices," let's look at the challenging task of relating consequences to children's behavior.

CHAPTER FIFTEEN

Determining the Right Consequences

Consequences, or the results of actions, affect us every day. To maximize learning, this chapter concentrates on how we can teach kids to be more conscious of the consequences of their actions.

The word "consequences" usually has a negative ring. We receive consequences for misbehavior, whereas we get rewards for positive behavior. In spite of the internal alarm that may be set off by the term "consequences," it only refers to results—which can be positive or negative.

Determining consequences is both an art and a science. We can carefully consider our decisions, using our heart and mind, our compassion and our reason. Remember also that consequences should help children take more responsibility for themselves and learn self-discipline. To help kids structure their environment, we can create interventions, which are actions plans to prevent problems. Whenever possible, this proactive approach should include children's participation in determining their consequences, while the adult retains veto power.

FROM BELIEFS TO CONSEQUENCES

Roger Bacon once explained, "To be commanded, Nature must be obeyed." In other words, as we understand the world

---

TABLE 15
FROM BELIEFS TO CONSEQUENCES

Thought/Belief

↓

Feelings

↓

Choices

↓

Decision

↓

Action

↓

Consequences

---

of our inner nature, we can develop ourselves to reach our potential. Understanding the "From Beliefs to Consequences" Table with its "natural" progression helps us discover our inner workings and how we—adults and children—express ourselves in the world.

Consequences help children realize that their choices and decisions count. Behind those decisions lie the beliefs, thoughts, and feelings that influence a decision (see Table 15). Previous sections in this book have explored dealing with these crucial aspects of kids' internal worlds.

Let's examine how a situation would play itself out from start to finish, from the time the thoughts and beliefs arise through the resulting feelings, choices, decisions, actions, and consequences. For example, a child does poorly on an exam, confirming her idea that school is "stupid" and difficult (belief). She expresses anger and frustration (feelings). She can try to improve or not (choices). She decides to give up (decision), plays instead of studying (action), and fails the next test (consequence), confirming her negative belief about school.

Here is another version of this example. A child does poorly on an exam and thinks she can get help (belief). She expresses concern and disappointment (feelings). She can try to improve or not (choices). She decides to get help from her peers or a tutor (action), and improves on the next test (consequence).

NATURAL AND LOGICAL CONSEQUENCES

Receiving a grade on a test is considered a "natural" consequence of the child's decisions about studying in school. Besides a "natural" result, consequences can also be selected as a "logical" follow-up to the child's behavior. This second kind of consequence is called a logical consequence, which is usually determined by someone who supervises the child's life. Logical consequences are "man-made" (or "woman-made"), intentionally created to address the original action.

Natural consequences "naturally" happen as a result of children's actions, such as a toy breaking because it was thrown. A logical consequence, on the other hand, needs to be carefully thought out so kids can learn from their mistakes. A logical consequence may be additional to a natural consequence. For example, if children continuously mishandle things, they may need to have limits set on how soon they can replace what they broke. This limit-setting would add a logical consequence (limiting access to items that have been carelessly broken) to a natural consequence (breaking the toy).

Here are other examples of logical consequences. If a child brings back a library book late because he misplaced it, he could pay a library fine from his allowance. This is a logical consequence. Or, if children are unfriendly, they may have to be separated from the other children, another "logical" consequence.

Consequences—both natural and logical—teach children how their behavior affects themselves and the world around them. Appropriate behavior helps themselves and others; impulsive and careless behavior hurts themselves and others.

To give consequences, you can map them out along the "Four Rs of Logical Consequences": Related, Respectful, Reasonable, and Revealed in Advance. Here is an example of how these four aspects work:

- **Related.** If the child hits another youngster, a "related" consequence could be going to a time-out area, away from others.

- **Respectful.** A "respectful" way to tell children of the consequence is in a calm, firm manner without belittling.

- **Reasonable.** It would be "reasonable" for the youngster to stay in the time-out area a limited amount of time, the length of time being based on the circumstances.

- **Revealed in Advance.** It also helps to "reveal in advance" that when children misbehave in a certain way, they will be given a time out to think about their behavior and be away from those they disturbed.

Developing Logical Consequences

Try involving children in determining appropriate consequences for their own actions. Sometimes my students have come up with better and more fitting consequences than I have.

> "So, Jason, what do you think should be the appropriate consequence of your taking Billy's cassette without permission?"
>
> "I should give it back, apologize, and let him borrow one of my tapes."
>
> "That's right," I agree, impressed with his thoughtful, responsible answer.

And you know Jason will live by the consequences he metes out for himself.

If Jason answers unreasonably, such as saying he does not need any consequences for his misdeed, I can respond, "No, that's not right. You know there will be consequences." Then I will be ready to offer my own logical consequences, which may be open to discussion, if they have not been set in advance.

Sometimes circumstances do catch us by surprise, and we are not prepared to give consequences. To resolve unexpected difficulties, be open to appropriate consequences naturally emerging from the situation. In any event, be mindful that you don't set a precedent for children arguing about the consequences as a way to avoid taking responsibility for themselves. The balance lies in finding suitable consequences, so kids can make better choices in the future.

Consequences serve to help us reflect on our lives and lead to improvements in the future. We may not like it when we receive a speeding ticket, but it sure makes us reflect on our behavior and slow down.

Help the child see how people in life—at work, on television, in the community—are continually reaping what they sow. If a worker is sloppily attired at a restaurant, ask how people feel having him or her around their food. What consequences could an unkempt waiter cause for the restaurant? What consequences might the worker receive? Ask what the young person would do if he or she were in that situation, both as a worker and as a supervisor.

In developing logical consequences remember to elicit the child's feelings. You want to acknowledge children's emotions while helping them find appropriate ways to share their inner worlds with you. Once you listen to kids' feelings, then you can proceed to discuss their thoughts, beliefs, and behavior. Explore how certain choices bring particular consequences. Help children realize how they are empowered to influence what happens to them, from their own thoughts, feelings, choices, and decisions.

★ TOOL 20 ★
Effective Consequences Checklist

When determining consequences for a child's actions, remember to:

✓ **Consider whether you are being too invasive.** For example, having the child share his diary can be invasive.

✓ **Explore the kid's feelings, thoughts, and beliefs, and how they relate to the situation at hand.**

✓ **Include the child's input in determining consequences.**

✓ **Incorporate the 4 R's of consequences: Related, Respectable, Reasonable, and Revealed in Advance.** Sometimes you don't plan for situations that arise, but with the other three aspects of consequences in place, children will usually accept the decision—despite some possible initial protest.

✓ **Make the consequences specific.** Children should know exactly what will happen if they follow or don't follow the rules.

✓ **Assess whether the consequence matters to the child.** If the child's consequence for neglecting homework is to miss television, he must care about the TV time he will miss. If he does not care, find something that will be more suitable, such as forgoing play time with friends until after homework is complete.

✓ **Set reasonable limits to a consequence.** For example, grounding the child for too long (say, a month) is counterproductive. Too harsh a consequence could foster the opposite effect you want. It might not quite qualify as cruel and unusual punishment, but such a long duration for grounding will probably breed more resentment than learning. Also, such situations end up being punishing to the adults involved as well.

✓ **Consider whether the consequences are enforceable.** You can enforce preventing alcohol and drugs in your home; but however much influence you may hold, you can't police the young person's behavior outside the home.

✓ **Follow through on your consequences.** Once you say it, you need to follow up, lest the message be that you don't really mean it. (Consistency is the subject of the next chapter.)

✓ **Remind children that "It's your choice."** Children should connect their choices with how they can take responsibility for their lives.

We all live in a world of consequences. Take a moment to consider a consequence—whether positive or negative—of something that you did recently. What did you learn from this experience? Just as such reflection can trigger understanding for you, you can help kids realize that facing consequences leads to growth and self-empowerment for their future. Consequences then become valuable, ongoing feedback, telling us how we are doing and where we are heading.

PLANNING INTERVENTIONS

How often do we give severe consequences because we are overly angry and frustrated? Consequences then turn into punishments, and after we calm down, we may realize that "the punishment doesn't fit the crime," so to speak.

Then it is time for some difficult decisions. One possibility is to stick with the questionable consequence, accepting that it may create further problems. It is debatable whether it is harder for us or for the kid to live with our poor decision. Preserving our poor judgment will probably breed resentment in the child, putting our authority and guidance in question.

Another way to deal with a poor decision we made about the child's misbehavior is to change the consequence to a fairer solution. You can find a better alternative for the youngster, which, as we mentioned earlier, the child can participate in creating. As Chapter 11 discussed, mistakes are our teachers and perfection is not the goal.

If we vacillate too much with the consequences, however, the child will be confused. We become inconsistent and unreliable. We send the message that we don't necessarily mean what we say. Why should the child believe us in the future if we have a history of changing our mind?

To become effective, consider having an action plan or intervention. An intervention helps on several levels:

- It prevents problems from occurring.
- It de-escalates problems when they happen.
- It reduces the chances that the problems will recur.

It is wise to think things out to accomplish effective and compassionate interventions. Before further restricting kids, we first want to discuss, explain, and listen. Find out from them more about the behavior that created the disturbance. Try to have *them* explain the negative impact of their actions, offering comments and questions to help them understand the problem. The goal is for children to internalize their understanding through their feelings, thoughts, beliefs, and the resulting actions.

Yet in spite of our best efforts, finest questions, and most effective listening, children will still continue to make mistakes, sometimes repeating the same errors we have so thoroughly discussed with them. This feedback indicates that further discussion, understanding, and approaches are needed. It also indicates that a further consequence, an intervention beyond discussing the problem, is in order. Such planning will help children learn from their experiences, allowing them to understand responsibility through appropriate and consistent structure.

Appropriate interventions steer children along the sometimes-shaky ground of childhood so they can reach the higher ground of maturity.

These measures are also needed to make others freer and safer from kids' disturbances. "Others," of course, may include you.

For instance, after you have discussed the importance of helping around the house, the child may still forget to do the chore. Then it is time to choose a reminder or restriction for the youngster. If that consequence turns out to be ineffective, then an alternative, perhaps more severe, consequence is needed.

Be aware of how much you increase the severity of the consequence. Are you increasing it in a moderate or an extreme amount? Does the child lose television privileges for the day, the week, or the month? What will get the message across in the fairest way?

Look at giving alternative consequences. Instead of losing television time, children can write an essay about their misbehavior, suggesting alternatives and stating what they have learned about the importance of doing chores. Also, consider denying the child a privilege until the chore is done. This puts the responsibility back on the young person.

Keep in mind that consequences should fit the action that created the disturbance. If the child is unfriendly to peers, the progression might be:

- A warning about the impact of unfriendly behavior, possibly discussing how it affects others.

- A time out to further remind the child of the problem and explore alternatives.

- An essay about personal responsibility.

- An extended period away from others since the child acted in an unfriendly, anti-social way.

Remember about relating the behavior to the consequence. For example, losing television time for avoiding chores does not clearly connect the consequence with what the child did. In other words, find a more "logical" way to give the consequence so it relates to the misbehavior. If neglecting chores creates disorder in the house, then maybe chores will need to be done during television time.

Crisis Intervention

There are also times for what author Michael Gurian calls "crisis intervention." Such exceptional circumstances occur during an emergency situation that faces the child. These are times when kids are in danger, calling for extreme measures to create safety and restore order. Examples of such threatening situations include a child playing in traffic, receiving abuse, or showing signs of suicidal behavior. The intervention would not be progressive; rather, the situation would call for a severe and immediate consequence, a solution that can restore safety as soon as possible.

Gurian cites a father who intervened with his sixteen-year-old son, who kept trying to seduce a thirteen-year-old girl. When the boy persisted, the father removed part of the engine from the boy's car. Although taking an unorthodox approach, the father felt compelled to stop his son from making such a serious, life-damaging mistake. His approach did succeed, and then the father returned the missing parts of his son's engine. A crisis intervention intends to help the young person realize the seriousness of the situation and find an immediate solution to avoid harm.

The American Justice System Model

To help plan interventions, the American justice system offers us an instructive model. If the child commits a "misdemeanor," to use a legal term, don't treat it as a major crime. If the child continues to commit misdemeanors, then a more severe consequence should be given. In effect, a pattern of offensive behavior warrants a greater consequence. The point is not to treat kids as though they are criminals, but to learn from how the justice system gives consequences to offenders.

However, child-rearing differs from penal justice in its emphasis on educating, not merely punishing, children. Kids need to understand distortions in their thinking and how these thoughts affect their behavior. Young people feel secure when they learn to respect rules and boundaries to keep them and others safe. When children sense a reasonable response by adults to their problems, they listen, learn, and grow.

Developing an Intervention Plan

Remember the advice that if Plan A doesn't work, it's time to try Plan B. Sometimes we get stuck, though, by replaying Plan A regardless of the poor results. So when using interventions with children, consider their effectiveness, and how to have alternatives available when one plan fails.

To be effective at any approach, you need to be consistent. Your consistency will allow you to test whether the intervention is actually working. If you are inconsistent, you cannot evaluate your approach. Inconsistency undermines your efforts because you can't tell if the problem lies with your approach, or with your inconsistent use of the approach, or both. This subject is further explored in the next chapter.

To determine an intervention plan, you can draw from examples in this chapter, use other tools in this book (see the Tool-list in the Introduction for an overview), and refer to your own experience. Remember that your kids are also valuable resources for developing interventions, which can help them respond favorably to the interventions they will experience. By including children's input, you develop their responsibility and decision-making as well.

Traditional interventions address problems after they occur. These approaches include:

- Nonverbal cues, such as pauses, disapproving looks, and head shakes.

- Verbal warnings, given respectfully and firmly.

- Loss of privileges or allowances.

- Time outs, taken in a separated safe area for a determined, reasonable time.

- Essays addressing the problem and finding solutions.

Many of the tools in this book help you prevent problems from occurring in the first place; the tools also help deal with problems once they occurred. In addition, all of the interventions described in this volume tend to minimize the recurrence of problems.

★ TOOL 21 ★
Finding the Lesson and the Alternatives

Here is another intervention to deal with problems. It is an easy-to-use process that focuses on finding alternatives for the child's behavior:

1. Start with acknowledging the child's error, and follow-up by asking, "What else could you have done?" Here are some examples:

   - "Instead of hitting your sister, what else could you have done?" (Talked to the parent, talked to her, taken a walk.)

   - "Instead of eating all the cookies, what else could you have done?" (Eaten fewer, shared them, asked before doing so.)

   - "Instead of teasing your sister, what else could you have done?" (Ignored her, talked with someone else, told her how I felt.)

   - Now it's your turn to find an example: "Instead of...."

2. You conclude this alternative-seeking process by asking the child, "What have you learned from this situation?"

This approach of helping kids find alternatives frees us from having to play the teacher, preacher, or savior with children. After some initial discomfort with our new freedom, we realize a weight has been lifted and our possibilities for effective communication with kids have grown.

The results of this alternative-seeking approach are telling. In discussing what they learned, I have heard children say, "It's better to talk things out than hit"; "I should ask before taking"; "I need to be more aware of myself." These are the kinds of answers we are seeking. Young people get to taste the sweetness of discovering their own answers. Their own discoveries make the learning internal, coming from the inside out. And that's what really counts.

In helping children find healthy alternatives, remember to ask these two questions:

1. What else could you have done?
2. What have you learned from this situation?

THE BEST LAID PLANS

As you know, problems often arise amid busy times, disrupting rhythms and routines. Kids' problems never seem to be at our convenience, which is another reason to prepare ourselves with plans to resolve conflicts. As the next chapter further discusses, any reasonable plan works better when used with consistency while still maintaining flexibility. Above all, keep in mind the individuality of the child.

I find that some intervention plan, however imperfect, is better than no plan. It is better to be prepared, knowing you can always adjust your plan and improve it or discard it. Plans provide a sense of order and security for children as well as yourself, provided that you administer the interventions with fairness and sensitivity. When all the approaches fail, it is time to go back to the drawing board, brainstorm, and ask for any available help from others in the face of those more difficult circumstances.

Alas, life cannot be fully planned out and measured, although we do gain security by being somewhat prepared, planning for what we can. Ultimately, we know that a child, like life itself, cannot be completely dealt with by planning, however helpful and constructive the designs.

CHAPTER SIXTEEN

Being Consistent

By exploring the topics in this book, you have boosted your self-awareness and self-confidence. Your relationships will continue to deepen by working with yourself and kids on the areas we have covered: expressing feelings, improving listening, developing honesty, and learning from mistakes.

To maintain what you have learned and further increase communication, we have come to another important step. You want to succeed when giving directions and setting limits with children. Becoming consistent with kids is a preventive medicine: It eliminates the need for many consequences and interventions.

This chapter examines aspects of consistency. It offers several tools to assert yourself with children while establishing a stable, nurturing environment for them. Let me start by sharing some advice I once received that made a big difference in my relationships with kids.

A PIECE OF ADVICE

When I was starting my teaching career, a principal once observed my classroom and advised me about teaching children: "First, tell them what you want them to do, and then have them do it."

No problem, I thought, I can easily adjust my approach with kids and use this feedback to improve my effectiveness. The principal's advice seemed obvious and filled with common sense. But as it turned out, I found the advice not so easy to apply. I did not realize the depth of this approach, and it took me some time to put it effectively into practice.

Years later, I can offer you this advice on how to apply the telling-them-what-to-do approach: Avoid becoming a drill sergeant. If your own effective way of communicating hasn't developed yet, be patient and persistent. You will find your own way of telling kids what you want them to do, while still giving them dignity and respect. You want to uphold your own word, honoring yourself, which will be reflected by children's respect to you. You then become a genuine authority for kids without resorting to authoritarianism.

Let's break the advice down into two parts: first "Tell kids what you want them to do," and then "have them do it." By following this approach in a flexible way, you can achieve consistency with kids, which makes everyone ultimately happy, despite some possible initial opposition.

Tell Them What You Want Them To Do

Before making a request to a child, it is wise to know the reason for giving the direction. This forethought prepares you for what can happen after your direction, such as kids' questions and protests. Here is the primary question to ask yourself when preparing to give a request: Am I willing to carry out this direction, including giving appropriate consequences, if the child refuses to follow? If the answer is "yes," you are on the right track for going ahead to make your request. If the answer is "no," it is time to do further preparation before proceeding.

Giving children a direction, or to put it politely, a request, explains what you expect from them. Keep in mind that children have the option to refuse, which takes them down the road of certain natural and logical consequences such as discussed earlier. They then must live with the consequences of their choice.

When we make requests of kids, they should be relevant and meaningful, in some way helpful to them and to others.

It might take some further explanation on how your making a request involving their time and energy will benefit them. But this is part of their ongoing education. For example: "It's time to take out the garbage?" "Why?" "Because it's nice to have a clean house that smells fresh and is free of bugs. And I'd like you to take it out before dinner, which is in half an hour."

We do our part. We give an explanation in a reasonable, patient tone, avoiding a power struggle. We state the reason for the request as simply and clearly as possible. We can also put a time frame on it.

So this concludes the first segment of this two-part bid for consistency, helping to structure the world we share with kids.

Now it is time for the second part, the all-important follow through on what we started.

And Then Have Them Do It

Follow through is essential to achieving consistency...or even partial results. We know that growing up includes testing boundaries. Kids watch closely to determine how much we mean what we say. Do we mean it every time, or just a certain percentage? Can kids get away with not taking out the garbage once in a while? Or can they delay the request, postponing the time we asked them to do it by taking out the trash after dinner? How much leeway is there? How serious are we about our requests to them? These considerations define the rules and the boundaries.

If we don't follow through on the consequences, children learn that we don't really mean what we say. They will then be motivated to question and test future situations. Our inconsistency also produces anxiety in both us and children.

The exception is when we determine that our decision is unworkable or unsuitable. Then it's time to acknowledge the error and explain why the consequences need to be changed. Kids will appreciate our honesty. They will also appreciate our effort to redress our own misjudgment that so affects their lives.

When giving a consequence, kids may protest. For instance, most of us aren't thrilled about taking out the trash. Yet young people will feel more secure knowing that we mean what we say. They then feel more protected, avoiding the anxiety created from our shifting positions. Like other directions that we give them, requesting them to take out the garbage is a reasonable thing for them to do, however much kids may grumble and complain.

Let us also see if we might have some of our own internal "garbage" to remove, so we can clearly "tell kids what we want them to do, and then have them do it." From our own self-examination, we can decide what we expect from kids and how we will follow through, which gives us the confidence to communicate clearly.

"JUST LET ME HOLD IT!"

When should you give the child a direction, knowing that you will need to follow up on it? To determine when to act, remember that if you give a child a direction, you set things in motion. You might need to go the distance so it gets done. Your request can involve some confrontation and resistance: resistance from the child in testing your directions and will and resistance from you in having to be thorough and persistent.

It is really up to you, so choose your directions carefully. You don't want to put so much effort into following through that you feel exhausted and the child feels defeated and resentful. In other words, you can win the battle and lose the war. You can overload children with directions or be too critical of how they accomplish the directions.

Let me share a story that deals with the kind of choices you may encounter.

In our Physical Education program, we were playing volleyball one day. Midway through the game, a thirteen-year-old boy named Joe left the playing area and came over to the sideline. Joe said he was feeling too winded and asthmatic, and that he wanted to rest. He stood on the sideline next to my teaching assistant, Randy, as I officiated a few yards away.

At first, Joe just looked on as his peers continue to play. Joe noticed that there were two extra volleyballs, one that Randy was holding and the other lying on the ground. Joe sauntered over to Randy, who was watching the ongoing game. Joe asked Randy if he could hold the ball. Randy told him "no," without offering any further explanation.

Joe persisted, "Just let me hold it!"

My assistant shook his head, indicating "no" again. A pause followed. Then Joe looked over at the other ball lying a few feet away on the ground. He picked it up and began to casually play with the ball as his peers continued with the game. Joe did not appear to be winded any more, and I watched to see what Randy would say to Joe. Randy was silent, allowing Joe to continue playing with the ball. Randy did not say anything about the student returning to the game, the activity he had left because he complained of being too winded.

I later questioned my assistant on why he initially refused to let Joe play with the volleyball on the sideline. (This is the "tell them what to do" part.) Randy answered that he did not trust Joe with the ball, and thought he would create a disturbance. I then asked Randy why he didn't say anything to Joe when the student proceeded to pick up the other ball. My assistant wasn't sure why he did not say anything to Joe. (This is the second part, following through by having them do what you told them to do—in this case, refraining from touching the ball.)

What message did the student receive from this experience? Joe learned that there are different ways to disregard an adult's directions. He succeeded in bypassing the adult's request, following his own impulses without restriction. Joe's behavior was reinforced by the adult's inconsistency. Here, then, is the prevention and the cure: If you're going to ask a kid not to hold the ball, you need to carry through, which may include confronting him about picking up another ball.

Let's take to heart the advice we sometimes give kids: Think before you speak and act. Is the direction worth giving to the youngster? It is better to refrain if you cannot follow through. If you think it is worth the effort, go for it. If you proceed with consistency, the child will feel more secure and guided, empowered to grow up more responsibly with healthy boundaries. The young person will also respect what you say, knowing that you will follow through.

I hope that Joe, the thirteen-year-old winded volleyball player, will someday grow up and offer clear, helpful, and reasonable directions when he guides children. To be effective, he, too, will have to learn how to be consistent and follow through on requests. The more people demonstrate appropriate consistency with him, the more he will know how to help others.

HAVING THE CHILD ASK ONLY ONCE

A common scene that involves consistency goes as follows:

> "Can I have that candy?"
> "No, it's almost dinner time."
> "Please, can I have that candy?"
> "I told you it's almost dinner."
> "What's for dinner?"
> "Lasagna and broccoli; you like those."
> "So please can I just have a little candy now?"
> "No…well, okay, just one piece."

Triumphant, the child eagerly receives the candy and consumes it. You hear a swallow and then the words, "Just one more piece?"

What's the problem with this scenario? What's the message the parent is sending to the youngster? The child is finding out if he persists and asks often enough, maybe he will get his way. It is a good bet. In our example, it took him three tries to get a yes. Even if he received another "no" on the third try, he might continue to ask, or beg, until his desire is granted. The eventual "yes" provides the incentive to keep trying on the next occasion. The message to the child is: If I pester enough, I might get my way. I have nothing to lose and definitely something to gain.

USA Today published some revealing statistics under the heading "Nagging Can Work." They showed how young kids' (ages three to eight) nagging made notable differences in their mothers purchasing such goods and services as movies, apparel, fast food, home videos, and tickets to Theme parks. The children's pestering made increases ranging from 20 to 40 percent in their getting what they wanted. Even though kids haven't read the statistics, their experience confirms that nagging works.

By being true to our word, we develop consistency and set a model for children.

There is truth in the idea that the squeaky wheel gets the grease. However, kids can become pretty squeaky. It is nice for them to develop persistence, but not at the expense of wearing us down, having us go back on our words to relieve the pressure from their nagging. Wavering, we then undermine what we say and the structure we provide for kids. If our words and structure are sound, shouldn't they be maintained, regardless of kids' impulses and desires?

In my classroom, I often hear new students make repeated requests after I have already told them an answer (which they didn't like). This nagging lets me know their approach has worked for them in the past.

For instance:

> "Phillip, can we do role-playing today?"
>
> "No, we did that yesterday. Today we are going to develop our writing skills by creating a story based on the role-play."
>
> "Can't we role-play?"
>
> I pause.
>
> Then I look into the student's eyes and firmly say, "Didn't I already answer that? I know it's not your first choice. Do you want me to repeat the same words over, or can you accept the decision so we can go on now?"

If the child knows you are consistent and won't yield to repeated demands, there is no incentive to keep asking. In fact, there is a disincentive to keep nagging you. By your tone, words, and body language, you let the child know he is being uncooperative and disruptive, rather than cooperative and helpful. There is a natural boundary set: You mean what you say the first time, and continued asking is not allowed. You are setting a standard, a pattern, and a structure for the child and for you.

By consistently maintaining what you say, you may need to just look wordlessly at the youngster after the second request. Your body language will convey the message: One request is enough.

★ TOOL 22 ★
Asked and Answered

There is a courtroom objection procedure that can help you limit kids' harassing requests. I am referring to when a lawyer interrupts the opposing lawyer's questioning of a witness by saying "Asked and answered." This procedure calls for an opposing lawyer to stop badgering a witness with repeated questions. The objection means that the lawyer has already asked the witness the question, and the witness has given an answer. By saying "Asked and answered," the first lawyer protects his witness from repeated questioning by the opposing lawyer. In other words, the legal system considers repetitive questioning of a witness a kind of harassment.

To prevent children from harassing you, you can use this "asked and answered" model for everyone's well-being. At times, kids argue like lawyers and certainly belabor repeated questions if we allow it. After you denied their first request, and they then repeat the same request, simply respond, "Asked and answered." Of course, you will need to explain what this term means. But after one or two clear explanations, children will quickly get the idea; and if you are consistent, the children will realize they have been given a cease-and-desist order from further nagging.

Saying "Asked and answered" serves as an efficient strategy, a way to prevent kids from badgering you. It saves you time and energy otherwise lost by youngsters' repeated questioning. On the other hand, when you give children the hope that you will eventually give in to their wishes, you reinforce their compulsive behavior. You make it worth their while to bother you in the hope that you will cave in. So next time they keep asking, you can say to their request, "Asked and answered."

FOUR KEYS TO CONSISTENCY

Here are four components to achieve consistency: predictability, firmness, flexibility, and appropriate nonverbal language. These aspects work together to help children transition through their developmental stages.

1. **Predictability.** I once asked a student of mine to take a time-out for his disruptive behavior. He began arguing with me, and then another student told the one who was protesting, "Forget it, don't waste your time. Mr. Mountrose isn't going to change his mind. You'll just make it worse by arguing." Ah...music to a teacher's ears!

2. **Firmness.** In addition to being predictable, consistency should be carried out with firmness. Your delivery needs to be decisive, without going to the extremes of either threatening or pleading. In other words, deliver requests with assertiveness. Avoid lecturing and power struggles; just calmly and squarely make your directions known to the young person. If the child refuses, you can respond, "That's your choice, but you know there will be a consequence. A positive consequence if you follow directions and a negative one if you don't."

   A cautionary note: As mentioned earlier, it is wise to know what consequences you will give. Or, if you need time to develop appropriate consequences, tell the child that there will be consequences coming. If possible, it is usually better to have thought them out ahead of time.

Firmly continue by saying: "If you do take out the garbage, I know you are being responsible. It tells me that I can trust you and give you certain privileges, like watching that show you have been asking me about. If you don't take out the garbage, we may need to delay dinner to take care of this matter...and you won't be able to see the show you wanted to watch."

3. **Flexibility.** To be consistent, you need to make reasonable requests. As discussed previously, account for your own misjudgments and include kids' feedback about the issue at hand. By evaluating your own requests, asserting what you feel, and considering children's input, you become flexible.

At times you may want to retract your directions, thinking it is not worth the effort to follow through, or perhaps it was a misguided request. For instance, maybe you remember it was not her turn to take out the trash. When you have second thoughts on your request after it has been made, consider the following:

- Think it through, including looking at the situation from the child's perspective. The young person wants to know whether you are going to follow through, and that the request was reasonable even if it is something he or she does not like to do. Although it was not the best request, follow through to achieve consistency if your conscience permits it.

- If you feel your request was too unreasonable or too difficult to follow through, it is time to redirect the child, explaining the reasons for your change.

- If you do make a mistake, admit your error. "Oh, I'm sorry, I forgot it was your sister's turn to take out the trash. I make mistakes too." This admission shows two admirable qualities: that you are both fair and vulnerable.

- Once you develop a pattern of consistency with your directions, you can afford to be a little lax on occasion, but don't make it a habit. Too much confusion with directions will undermine your consistency. Frequent changes in directions with kids create anxiety for them, which in turn can cause them to resist your requests. If you find yourself wavering too much, re-examine why you gave the direction in the first place.

4. **Appropriate Nonverbal Language.** Check nonverbal signals when making requests. What is your body posture? Are you standing upright, looking the child in the eye? Or are you slumped, looking away, distracted by another activity when making the request? Or are you hovering over the child, pointing your finger at her in a menacing fashion? How is your tone of voice? Is your voice clear and even-toned? Or are you yelling or mumbling?

★ TOOL 23 ★
Developing Consistency

To evaluate and develop your consistency with kids, you can use the following method. Consider using it for different directions you have given children.

1. Recall a time when you gave a direction to a child. What was your intent and goal in giving this direction? For example, I asked her to play more quietly because it was disturbing to her brother and to me. She also was playing too recklessly.

2. Describe the tone of your voice and body posture when you delivered your request. Try to recall the words you used and your feelings at the time.

3. Describe how the youngster responded to your direction. What was her body language; what were her words, her feelings?

4. What was your follow through on the direction? Rate its effectiveness: use words and/or a number rating from one to ten (ten being the most effective).

5. Did you accomplish your original intent as described in step one?

6. Upon reflection, was it a worthwhile direction to give and follow through on?

7. If desired, how would you improve next time?

8. Take a possible request you might make to a child. Imagine how you would deliver it; consider your verbal and nonverbal language. How would you follow through on your direction?

9. What have you learned from this exercise?

REVIEWING CONSISTENCY

This chapter has offered different ways to achieve consistency with young people. It has illustrated the principle of telling children what we want them to do, and then having them do it. Remember, though, that before responding to a situation where a child tests our will, it is worth the effort to be clear on what we want and then generally stick to it. Let's think through our decisions and be sensitive on how they affect the child.

To further help with consistency, this chapter dealt with how to limit the number of times children make the same request. The "Asked and Answered" tool helps concisely deliver our message for kids to stop repeating their requests.

The chapter went on to describe the four keys to consistency: predictability, firmness, flexibility, and nonverbal language. And this section concluded with a tool on evaluating and developing our own consistency. Let's now turn to something that also affects our consistency and effectiveness with children: complaining.

CHAPTER SEVENTEEN

Dealing with Complaining

One of the many things children learn how to do is complain. Like repeating requests, this annoying habit can easily be picked up by kids. Where could they have learned such an unpleasant habit? Once again, we need to hold up the mirror to ourselves and listen to how often we complain and nag around children. We also need to consider how we respond to kids' complaints.

Complaining is like bad breath: It pollutes the air, it's much too common, and no one likes it. Complaining can also be symptomatic of other problems.

Here is one way I deal with complaints in the classroom. When a child complains about the assignment—"Oh no, not math!"—I sometimes look around the room and then say, "I could have sworn I just heard a complaint. Well, maybe it was nothing; I probably was just imagining it." I also offer students appropriate ways to express legitimate complaints. Young people need to recognize the seriousness of their complaints and learn appropriate ways to let their concerns be known.

Most adults realize it is *not* helpful to blurt out in front of the whole office how fed up they are with a task. To find appropriate ways to express frustration, we as adults can find someone in authority who will listen to our problems. A process of examination can begin, which would hopefully include any needed correction.

So, too, for children. The time to express difficulties is in private, not as a grandstand announcement. Public complaining creates a negative atmosphere and invites other kids to follow suit. In my class, if a student has genuine troubles that need addressing—a subject is too difficult, or a disturbance from a peer—he can see me at break, and I will be glad to discuss it. Then I can acknowledge the student, and possibly seek alternatives.

Generally, a personal problem does not justify taking up the whole class time. Depending on the situation, I might seek out the student to learn in private more of what bothers him. Usually, though, a complaining comment stems from some personal irritation or frustration, which vanishes by the break when there is time to talk privately.

An exception to handling problems in private includes the student's having a complaint that could improve the lesson. "Do we have to work in that boring spelling book again? Can't we have a spelling bee?" This suggestion could benefit the whole class, if the teacher can see get past the blunt criticism.

Keep in mind that the complaint may be more than a bad habit. Complaining can signal a problem with the young person's underlying feelings, thoughts, and beliefs. Brainstorming possible solutions with the child can help.

On the one hand, complaining is a bad habit, reflecting poor social skills and impulse control. On the other hand, complaints can indicate that something is out of balance, and the child's thoughts and feelings need to be heard. By helping the child deal with genuine problems, the young person will become more resourceful, eliminating many future complaints. Children then grow more aware, which resolves legitimate concerns and reduces impulsive comments. It certainly makes it much nicer to be with kids as well.

★ TOOL 24 ★
The "I Know" Technique

Have you ever wanted a shortcut to stop kids' nagging requests and complaints? Here is a "quick fix" you can easily put to use. It may not permanently solve the problem, but it gets you past the immediate nagging and complaining, at least temporarily. If the situation warrants more attention, this technique can give you time until you can more deliberately address any of the child's underlying issues and concerns. Many of the previously described tools can be used for those more in-depth discussions.

The "I Know" tool offers a simple, concise approach that works well on several fronts. Consider using this technique for the following:

- When you need to remind children of some responsibility that they resist.

- When you need to deny them something they want.

This technique addresses a common complaint by kids, which was discussed in Chapter 6: not getting their way. The approach also lets you convey with brevity that the subject is not up for discussion. In effect, it lets you be proactive, avoiding arguments for various situations.

The "I Know" technique can be used when the child complains about not wanting to do something. Here is how this tool works: Simply respond to the child's remark by saying, "I know that, but it's time for [whatever is the necessary action that the child is resisting]." Or "I know that, but you know [give the reason why the child can't get his way]."

Here are some examples to show how this approach works. Remember to deliver your "I know" comments in a firm but caring manner.

- Child: "I'm tired. I don't want to go to school."
  You: "I know, but it's time to go to school now."

- Child: "I can't stand cleaning my room."
  You: "I know you don't like to do that, but it's time to clean your room."

- Child: "I don't like doing that."
  You: "I know that, but you know it needs to be done."

- Child: "I want that CD."
  You: "I know you wish you could have it right now, but we'll have to wait until I can afford it."

- Create your own example:

Sometimes you might have to repeat the "I know" response to make sure it is heard and accepted. The goal is to prevent the child from continually petitioning you, the kind of nagging and complaining previously discussed.

This technique is more than just repeating your request like a tape loop that replays itself. It adds the important component of validating, however briefly, what the child has said by saying "I know" in your response.

Realize that this technique is hardly a foolproof solution for every situation. But it does come in handy, often avoiding power struggles. The "I know" approach also readily validates kids' positions when they don't get what they want, while still maintaining your ground. Of course, sometimes more discussion is in order. But there are plenty of occasions when time is short and things need to be done. The "I know" approach can help you and the child get them done quickly.

This part of the book, "Making Growth Choices," offers many ways to help you and the children in your life. The next chapter helps consolidate your efforts to get better results.

CHAPTER EIGHTEEN

Getting Results

The jazz musician Miles Davis noted that "sometimes you have to play a long time to be able to play like yourself." In my journey, "to play like yourself" meant learning how to become a quality teacher and communicator, which took time and particular effort. At the start of my career, I noticed that my teaching produced average results compared with the results that experienced teachers were getting. They had better classroom management and rapport with kids, better communication. I was trying hard and doing many things right, but where was I going wrong? What was missing?

I searched to find those missing pieces, to improve the quality of my teaching and relationships with children. I discovered that you could be doing a majority of things right—careful planning, innovative lessons, good record-keeping, deep commitment to children—and still not have excellent results.

It seemed that you could be getting six out of ten things right, a majority, but you really need eight or nine out of ten to be effective. At the time, I was frustrated that my efforts seemed to fall short, producing disappointing results.

But I persisted. Eventually my efforts led me to the conclusion Bruno Bettelheim had reached in *Love Is Not Enough*:

> It is not even enough to do the right thing at the right moment; it must also be done with emotions that belong to the act. Again and again in our work we have found that what counted was not so much the hard facts as the feelings and attitudes that went with them.

Aha! It is not only about how many areas you cover, but also how you cover the areas.

Finding those "feelings and attitudes" took time and many trials and errors for me. Eventually I learned how to make lemonade out of my lemons. Along the way, I had to find alternatives to using authoritarian solutions when I got stuck with a child or a class. I had to overcome anxieties about dealing with children. My fears included losing control of the class and losing control of myself.

To learn from mistakes and find out about my shortcomings, I turned to examining my own thoughts, feelings, and beliefs. This self-examination helped my own development, translating into more effective communication with kids. Then much of the knowledge I had learned through dealing with children became more my own, naturally adapted to my style. I was able to relax and be more myself. My comfort level with myself rose, helping me find the solutions I once had so anxiously sought at the beginning of my teaching career.

I want to share with you a challenging situation that occurred in my more mature phase of teaching.

"I COULD HURT MYSELF"

This story illustrates how to get quality results, which involves dealing with your own feelings and thoughts as well as the child's.

During a lesson one day, Bobby, a five-foot-ten-inch, 210-pound fourteen-year-old, suddenly walked out of my class. He had left the classroom without permission, and once he had left, he refused to take directions from my assistant George. Bobby moved randomly outside the classroom around a kitchen area. He was acting giddy, impulsive, and possibly dangerous, particularly in light of his past reckless behavior. George kept giving him directions to calm down and go to the time-out space, the designated area for students who were experiencing difficulty. Bobby continued to shuffle around the kitchen, acting like the situation was something of a game and a challenge.

Bobby smiled and moved away from George. If things escalated further, Bobby knew that he would be "escorted" to the time-out area. This meant putting hands-on—a staff person (or two) holding him by the elbow—as he would be walked to the designated safe area.

By the time I came out of the classroom into the tense scene, Bobby was sitting on the counter top next to the stove. George told him in a stern, confrontational tone, "Come on, Bobby, you know you need to go to the time-out area." George took a step closer to Bobby. "You know you can do it on your own; we don't want to have to put hands on you."

"If you do, you'll be sorry," Bobby said, acting part imp and part menace. Then he turned on one of the burners and put his hand close to it. He grinned as if he was about to come unglued. At this point, he noticed my presence in the room. Looking at me, he said, "Phil, I could hurt myself."

I intentionally responded in a calm, slow manner. "You could. Bobby, you seem a little upset. Let's go over to the couch and talk about it." I motioned with my head for him to come with me, and I started to walk toward the couch. Fortunately, Bobby got off the countertop and followed me.

On the sofa, I talked in a quiet voice to him about his feelings and asked him the consequences of continuing this behavior. I also asked him what should be the consequences of the actions he had already taken. He admitted his anxiety, talked about family concerns, and acknowledged the dangers of his action. He also assigned himself a reasonable consequence for his reckless actions.

There may be occasions when we need to physically hold a youngster for his and others' safety. But following my heart, I sensed this was not one of those times. In my earlier career, I probably would have acted like George, my assistant, in this situation. I would have been doing most of the right things — being assertive about boundaries, offering warnings, strictly following program procedures—and probably would have mediocre results. But by going within, being in the moment, getting in touch with my feelings and the student's, I was able to use the school rules, boundaries, and consequences to reach a positive result.

Doing enough things right and in the right way improved the outcome of the situation. Here is what made the difference with Bobby: sensing when to follow him, sensing when to lead him, and using an appropriate attitude.

Getting results has two parts: First have a sense of what to do, and then follow through on your inner prompting. The good news is that everyone can get results; it just takes some knowledge, effort, and experience—and learning from mistakes along the way.

★ TOOL 25 ★
Improving Your Results

To improve your results with children, consider the following:

- Identify an area where you have difficulty with kids, such as having them follow directions.

- Evaluate what you have attempted so far. How consistently did you try this approach? What worked and what needs improvement?

- Locate resources to help you find solutions and come up with an action plan. Resources include meditation and prayer, advice from those experienced in the area, and reference material.

- Map out a new action plan. You can write it down to further clarify it.

- After using your action plan, record the results. If unsuccessful, give it time, consistent application, and further evaluation.

- Realize that getting results is both a goal and a process. It can take time to resolve situations. This improving-your-results tool allows opportunities for everyone to learn and grow.

Getting results is a matter of both the quantity and quality of your efforts. It requires patience and persistence. Getting results expresses your love and devotion, and it develops the will to fulfill your needs and desires.

Trust that your intent will bring results. Know that you can provide care and structure for kids.

YOUR POSITIVE MOMENTUM

This part of the book has covered a wide range of "Growth Choices." Consider the gains you have made and the areas you wish to revisit. You have tips and tools on helping children to be honest, express remorse, and find their own answers. You can help children discriminate in courage and risk-taking. Using appropriate consequences, you have more resources to help kids structure their environments and develop self-discipline. You understand how to reduce children's complaints and guide them by being more consistent with your words and actions.

In the final pages of this book, we examine how raising consciousness is crucial to our present and future.

Increasing Awareness

We are but one thread within it [the web of life].
Whatever we do to the web, we do to ourselves.
All things are bound together. All things connect.

- CHIEF SEATTLE

Author Deepak Chopra talked with Rosa Parks about her courageous action in 1955 on an Alabama public bus where she refused to give up her seat to a white man. Chopra asked her, "Do you have anger about the way you, and everyone you knew, were treated?" The quiet woman, whose historic act transformed the civil rights movement, responded, "No. Everybody was doing the best they could from their level of consciousness. What we have to do is improve consciousness."

The answer to just about all of our problems comes down to increasing our awareness. Awareness is the goal and the way to reach the goal. As we raise our consciousness, we become more inclusive of others and able to accomplish our lives' purposes. It connects us to what is around us and what is inside us.

Mahatma Gandhi counseled that if we want peace in the world, we need to start with the children. To do this, I would also add that we need to examine ourselves, finding ways to connect with our own wholeness. Then we will be in a better place to guide and mentor our kids, along with learning from them. The more we pursue our own development, the more we can help kids with their development.

It's good to take a deep breath... and allow our awareness to expand. As more things come to the light, we grasp more of the bigger picture and how we fit in.

DEVELOPING MORE CONSCIOUSNESS

As we grow, the old ways of doing things eventually don't work any more. At first, these changes can cause confusion in our lives. We wonder how to proceed through the void that was once filled with familiar habits and approaches. To understand how to progress, we can examine our own childhood, realizing that we acquired defenses for the hurt we didn't know how to deal with at the time. Those defended areas cover wounds that patiently await an opportunity to be recognized and healed. By dealing with these afflicted parts of ourselves, we become more whole, successfully completing the developmental stages wherein the difficulties occurred. Free of the chains from our past, we are able to live in the present and look toward the future, motivated by our dreams and goals of a better world.

As we give ourselves and our children the love and coping skills to release that pain, everyone becomes more alive. We are better able to live life and help others. Our efforts and awareness bring renewal; we transform ourselves by discovering new ways to understand ourselves and our kids.

We find underneath our defenses and wounds a wonderful heart and soul, a unique being that yearns for growth, freedom, and fulfillment. We all deserve that connection to who we really are, and ultimately there is no one stopping us except ourselves. As we discover our truth—and teach it to our children—what a world we will create!

THE JOURNEY CONTINUES

As your toolbox has now grown, the next step can be to further use the tools in this book, improving your skills and abilities. Applying the tools and information will continue to help dissolve negative patterns and raise the quality of your life. Know that you can now do more of what you really want and be more of who you really are. Such invaluable realizations will be wonderfully transmitted to the children in your life.

This book is intended to spark your awareness so more consciousness can grow in you. Not only can you now access more knowledge, you can also access more resources within yourself. Consider revisiting the tool-list overview in the Introduction to determine which areas are most important for you at this time.

As you use this book's communication approaches, you will generate your own tips and tools for further communication with children, adults, and yourself. As you get through to yourself, in all your vastness and mystery, you will also be getting through to the kids in your life. They will then be better prepared someday to get through to the kids in their lives.

Selected Bibliography

Bayard Robert, and Jean Bayard. *How to Deal with Your Acting-Up Teenager*. New York: M. Evans & Company, 1983. A brilliant and practical approach to sorting out and dealing with a host of problems, based on the Bayard's family-counseling practice.

Bettelheim, Bruno. *Love Is Not Enough*. New York: Avon Books, 1971. Dr. Bettelheim's work with disturbed children in the 1940s holds lessons for us today.

Bilodeau, Lorraine. *The Anger Workbook*. Minneapolis, Minnesota: CompCare Publishers, 1992. A valuable resource on this complex subject.

Bradshaw, John. *Healing the Shame That Binds You*. Deerfield Beach, Florida: Health Communications, 1988.

—. *Bradshaw On: The Family*. Deerfield Beach, Florida: Health Communications, 1988. John Bradshaw blends personal experience, research, and strategies to help understand the family breakdown and how it can be repaired.

Chiles, Pila. *The Secrets & Mysteries of Hawaii: A Call to the Soul*. Deerfield Beach, Florida: Health Communications, 1995. A wonderful account of the spiritual history and uniqueness of Hawaiian culture.

Chopra, Deepak. "From Deepak." *Deepak Chopra's Infinite Possibilities Newsletter*, Volume 2. Issue 11. 1998: 1-2. An engaging newsletter from a Renaissance man, who offers spiritual and health advice as well as interviewing others of like mind.

Clark, Jean, and Connie Dawson. *Growing Up Again: Parenting Ourselves, Parenting Our Children*. Center City, Minnesota: Hazelden, 1998. A thoughtful collection of well-formatted information to structure and care for yourself and kids.

Claro, Joe. *Random House Book of Jokes and Anecdotes*. New York: Random House, 1994.

Coles, Robert. *The Moral Intelligence of Children: How to Raise a Moral Child*. New York: Random House, 1997. A compassionate and insightful work on how children learn morals.

Davis, Laura. *The Courage to Heal Workbook: For Women and Men Survivors of Child Sexual Abuse*. New York: Harper & Row, 1990. An excellent workbook providing thought-provoking and self-reflective approaches for anyone who experienced childhood abuse. It can also be used by anyone to help understand troubling experiences while growing up.

Elgin, Suzette Haden. *The Gentle Art of Communicating with Kids*. New York: John Wiley & Sons, 1996. A detailed analysis of how to use and improve language.

Ginott, Haim. *Between Parent & Child*. New York: Avon Books, 1965.

—. *Teacher & Child: A Book for Parents and Teachers*. New York: Avon Books, 1972. Ginott's books are filled with common-sense advice on a variety of important subjects.

Goleman, Daniel. *Emotional Intelligence: Why It Can Matter More Than I*. New York: Bantam Books, 1995. Goleman gives an overview of how emotional intelligence extensively affects society, including parenting, marriage, careers, and health.

Gottman, John. *The Heart of Parenting: Raising an Emotionally Intelligent Child*. New York: Simon & Schuster, 1997. Drawing on two, ten-year studies of more than 120 families, Professor Gottman shows how Emotion Coaching can make a critical difference in the lives of children.

Gurian, Michael. *The Wonder of Boys*. New York: Tarcher/Putnam, 1996.

—. *A Fine Young Man*. New York: Tarcher/Putnam, 1998. Both books by this author give careful analysis and research on how to understand and nurture boys.

Hendrix, Harville, and Helen Hunt. *Giving the Love That Heals: A Guide for Parents*. New York: Pocket Books, 1997. Groundbreaking connections on how parenting kids is about healing yourself.

Imber-Black, Evan. *The Secret Life of Families: Truth-Telling, Privacy, and Reconciliation in a Tell-All Society*. New York: Bantam Books, 1998. An important area for study, which by definition is hidden from our awareness.

Johnson, Luanne. *School Is Not a Four-Letter Word: How to Help Your Child Make The Grade*. New York: Hyperion, 1997. A wise teacher offers a variety of ways to help children succeed in school.

Kundtz, David. *Stopping: How to Be Still When You Have to Keep Going*. Berkeley, California: Conari Press, 1998. A valuable study of what the author calls "Stopping," an easy-to-use alternative to traditional meditation.

Mountrose, Phillip. *Getting Thru to Kids: Problem Solving with Children Ages 6 to18*. Sacramento, California: Holistic Communications, 1997. The first book in the series, focusing on a practical five-step approach to help kids create positive beliefs, improving their safety, honesty, trust, friendship, and school attitudes.

Pearsall, Paul. *The Heart's Code: Tapping the Wisdom and Power of Our Heart Energy*. New York: Broadway Books, 1998. An insightful psychoneuroimmunologist blends the theory and science behind findings about the heart with profound implications for us all.

Pearson, Carol. *Awakening the Heroes Within: Twelve Archetypes to Help Us Find Ourselves and Transform the World*. Harper-SanFrancisco, 1991. Important knowledge about how to understand archetypes, universal energy patterns, that can be used to fulfill our potential.

Ruiz, Don Miguel. *The Four Agreements: A Toltec Wisdom Book*. San Rafael, California: Amber Allen, 1997. A shamanic Indian approach for transcending limiting beliefs and establishing a liberating code of conduct.

Vernon, Ann. *Thinking, Feeling, Behaving: An Emotional Education Curriculum for Children*. Champaign, Illinois: Research Press, 1989. Although designed for grades 1-6, this excellent workbook can be selectively used with older children.

Index

About the Author

Phillip Mountrose has educated kids of all ages for over twenty years. He has a master's degree in education from the University of Massachusetts, a special education certification, and a master's in TV Production from UCLA. He has taught kindergarten through grade 12 classes, including special education with emotionally disturbed adolescents. He has also created instructional videos on work attitudes for young people entering the job market. In addition to his educational background, Phillip Mountrose developed his unique approach through working many years with individuals and groups in the area of self-help.

His first book in the "Getting Thru" series was the award-winning *Getting Thru to Kids: The Five Steps to Problem Solving with Children Ages 6 to 18*. He also co-wrote with Jane Mountrose *Getting Thru to Your Emotions with EFT: Tap into Your Hidden Potential with the Emotional Freedom Techniques*.

Phillip Mountrose warmly welcomes your communication, especially your experiences, insights, challenges, and successes with the interactive tools in this volume. Also, for more information about scheduling personal sessions, consultations, speaking engagements, and seminars contact:

Phillip Mountrose
P.O. Box 41152, Sacramento, CA 95841-0152
e-mail: kids@gettingthru.org
www.gettingthru.org

Resources

BOOKS FROM HOLISTIC COMMUNICATIONS

Getting Thru to Kids: The Five Steps to Problem Solving with Children and Teenagers **by Phillip Mountrose**
Learn the key steps to problem solving with children, improving trust, honesty, school attitude, and friendships. Jack Canfield, co-author of *Chicken Soup for the Soul* series, says, "This wonderful little book offers a simple and effective method to create peace and harmony in the home and high self-esteem in your children."

Getting Thru to Your Emotions with EFT: Tap into Your Hidden Potential with the Emotional Freedom Techniques **by Phillip and Jane Mountrose**
By simply tapping on a series of points on the body, you can use these extraordinary techniques to clear stuck emotions and self-defeating patterns, producing profound breakthroughs. An essential self-help resource to create more joy, love, and freedom in your life.

The Holistic Approach to Eating: Lose Extra Weight and Keep It Off for Life **by Jane Mountrose**
This 82-page booklet gives you the keys to losing and maintaining your weight for life. Learn the reasons traditional diets fail and techniques that really work. Make real progress and feel good about yourself.

AUDIO TAPES AND VIDEO TAPES

Getting Thru to Kids: Problem-Solving with Children Ages 6 to 18: **Two Audio Tapes.** This audio set gives you the essence of Phillip Mountrose's award-winning book, read by the author. Uplifting and easy to follow, great for deepening your communication skills.

Getting Thru to Your Emotions with EFT: **Video Tapes.**
These two tapes present the processes described in the book through real examples and demonstrations. Seeing the techniques in action will help with your timing, precision, and presentation. The procedures have commentaries by Phillip and Jane Mountrose. Tape One presents the EFT processes. Tape Two presents the GTT processes.

Getting Thru to Your Emotions with EFT : **Two Audio Tapes.** This two-tape set provides guided versions of the GTT processes presented in this book, with background music. These tapes allow you to sit or lie back and relax, while we guide you through each of the processes.

Centering and Reaching for the Light: **One Audio Tape.**
This lucid tape explores the power and importance of becoming centered in your True Self, your Soul, and the journey toward embodying it in your daily life. Includes a powerful meditation that you can use regularly. Narrated by Jane Mountrose.

Ordering information for the above materials is located at the end of this book.

Order Form

ITEM	QUANTITY	COST
Tips and Tools for Getting Thru to Kids: Book $ 12.95	_____	_____
Getting Thru to Kids: Problem-Solving With Children Ages 6-18: Book $11.95	_____	_____
Getting Thru to Kids: 2-tape Audio $16.95	_____	_____
Getting Thru to Your Emotions: Book $13.95	_____	_____
Getting Thru to Your Emotions: Two Audio Tapes $16.95	_____	_____
Getting Thru to Your Emotions Videos: Part 1: The EFT Techniques: Video $24.95	_____	_____
Part 2: The GTT Techniques: Video $24.95	_____	_____
Part 1 and Part 2 Videos together $39.95	_____	_____
Holistic Approach to Eating: Booklet $10	_____	_____
Centering and Reaching the Light: Audio $10	_____	_____

Subtotal _____

US Shipping $3.00 first item, $.50 each additional item _____
(for shipping outside United States, add $7)

California residents please add 7.75% for sales tax _____

AMOUNT ENCLOSED _____

Order Form continued on the next page